Instant Pot®
QUICK & EASY

pil

Publications International, Ltd.

Pictured on the front cover *(clockwise from top left):* Lemon Blueberry Oatmeal *(page 12),* Pesto Turkey Meatballs *(page 104),* Simple Rotisserie Chicken *(page 80)* and Irish Beef Stew *(page 124).*

Pictured on the back cover *(clockwise from top left):* Pancake Breakfast Casserole *(page 22),* Split Pea Soup *(page 70),* Asian Chicken and Noodles *(page 73),* Big Chocolate Chip Cookie *(page 217),* Brussels Sprouts in Orange Sauce *(page 194)* and Chickpea Tikka Masala *(page 162).*

ISBN: 978-1-64558-388-2

Manufactured in China.

8 7 6 5 4 3 2 1

CONTENTS

INTRODUCTION TO INSTANT POT®

Welcome to the wonderful world of Instant Pot cooking!

Although the current craze makes it seem like a new invention, pressure cooking has actually been around for a few hundred years. Many people grew up hearing stories of pressure cooker catastrophes—exploding pots and soup on the ceiling—but those days are long gone. There have been great changes and improvements in recent years to make modern pressure cookers completely safe, quiet and easy to use.

Kale and Roasted Pepper Frittata *(page 24)*   Italian Beef Sandwiches *(page 128)*

What exactly is a pressure cooker?

It's a simple concept: Liquid is heated in a heavy pot with a lid that locks and forms an airtight seal. Since the steam from the hot liquid is trapped inside and can't evaporate, the pressure increases and raises the boiling point of the contents in the pot, and these items cook faster at a higher temperature. In general, pressure cooking can reduce cooking time to about one third of the time used in conventional cooking methods—and typically the time spent on pressure cooking is hands off. (There's no peeking or stirring when food is being cooked under pressure.)

What makes the Instant Pot different?

The Instant Pot is a versatile electric multi-cooker that can be a pressure cooker, rice cooker, slow cooker, steamer and yogurt maker. The cooking programs you'll find on the control panel are convenient shortcuts for some foods you may prepare regularly (rice, beans, etc.) which use preset times and cooking levels. But in these pages we'll explore the basics of pressure cooking with recipes that primarily use the Pressure Cook or Manual button along with customized cooking times and pressure levels. These simple and delicious dishes will inspire you to use your Instant Pot daily and create your own Instant Pot magic!

Instant Pot Components

The **exterior pot** is where the electrical components are housed. It should never be immersed in water; to clean it, simply unplug the unit, wipe it with a damp cloth and dry it immediately.

The **inner pot** holds the food and fits snugly into the exterior pot. Made of stainless steel, it is removable, and it can be washed by hand or in the dishwasher.

The **LED display** shows a time that indicates where the pressure cooker is in a particular function. The time counts down to zero from the number of minutes that were programmed. (The timing begins once the machine reaches pressure.) For Keep Warm and Yogurt functions, the time counts up.

The **pressure release valve** is on top of the lid and is used to seal the pot or release steam. To seal the pot, move the valve to the Sealing position; to release pressure, move the valve to the Venting position. This valve can pop off to clean, and to make sure nothing is blocking it.

The **float valve** controls the amount of pressure inside the pressure cooker and indicates when pressure cooking is taking place. The valve rises once the contents of the pot reach working pressure; it drops down when all the pressure has been released after cooking.

The **anti-block shield** is a small stainless steel cage found on the inside of the lid that prevents the pressure cooker from clogging. It can be removed for cleaning.

The **silicone sealing ring** underneath the lid helps create a tight seal to facilitate pressure cooking. The sealing ring has a tendency to absorb strong odors from cooking (particularly from acidic ingredients); washing it regularly with warm soapy water or in the dishwasher will help these odors dissipate, as will storing your Instant Pot with the lid ring side up. If you cook both sweet and savory dishes frequently, you may want to purchase an extra sealing ring (so the scent of curry or pot roast doesn't affect your rice pudding or crème brûlée). Make sure to inspect the ring before cooking—if it has any splits or cracks, it will not work properly and should be replaced.

Instant Pot Cooking Basics

Every recipe is slightly different, but most include these basic steps. Read through the entire recipe before beginning to cook so you'll know what ingredients to add and when to add them, which pressure level to use, the cooking time and the release method.

1. **Sauté:** Many recipes call for sautéing vegetables or browning meat at the beginning of a recipe to add flavor. (Be sure to leave the lid off in this step.)

2. Add the ingredients as the recipe directs and secure the lid, making sure the arrow mark on the lid is aligned with the "close" mark and lock icon on the rim of the outside pot. Turn the pressure release valve to the Sealing position.

3. Select Pressure Cook or Manual, then choose the pressure level. The default setting is high pressure, which is what most recipes in this book use. To change to low pressure, use the Pressure Level or Adjust button. To set the cooking time, use the + and - buttons. The Instant Pot will start automatically.

4. Once the pressure cooking is complete, use the pressure release method directed by the recipe. There are three types of releases:

Natural release:

Let the pressure slowly release on its own, which can take anywhere from 5 to 25 minutes (but is typically in the 10- to 15-minute range). The release time will be shorter for a pot that is less full and longer for one that is more full. When the float valve lowers, the pressure is released and you can open the lid.

Quick release:

Use a towel or pot holder to manually turn the pressure valve to the Venting position immediately after the cooking is complete. (Be sure to get out of the way of the steam before turning the valve.) It can take up to 2 minutes to fully release all the pressure; the float valve will drop down when all the pressure is released.

A combination of natural and quick release:

The recipe will instruct you to let the pressure release naturally for a certain amount of time (frequently for 10 minutes), and then do a quick release as directed.

Tips, Tricks, Dos and Don'ts

- Read the manual before beginning. There may be features you won't use, but it will eliminate some beginner's confusion, and it can help you understand how the Instant Pot works—and see all its possibilities. Models also change over time, so the manual can provide the best information about the buttons and functions of your pot. (Note that the terms "Pressure Cook" and "Manual" are interchangeable.)

- Don't overfill the pot—the total amount of food and liquid should not exceed the maximum level marked on the inner pot. Generally it is best not to fill the pot more than two thirds full; when cooking foods that expand during cooking such as beans and grains, do not fill it more than half full.

- Make sure there is always some liquid in the pot before cooking because a minimum amount is required to come up to pressure (the amount differs between models). However, if the recipe contains a large quantity of vegetables or meats, you may be able to use a bit less since these ingredients will create their own liquid.

- Always check that the pressure release valve is in the right position before you start pressure cooking. The food simply won't get cooked if the valve is not in the Sealing position because there will not be enough pressure in the pot.

- Never try to force the lid open after cooking—if the lid won't open, that means the pressure has not fully released. (As a safety feature, the lid remains locked until the float valve drops down.)

- Save the thickeners for after the pressure cooking is done. Pressure cooker recipes often end up with a lot of flavorful liquid left in the pot when cooking is complete; flour or cornstarch mixtures can thicken these liquids into delicious sauces. Use the Sauté function while incorporating the thickeners into the cooking liquid, and then cook and stir until the desired consistency is reached.

- Keep in mind that cooking times in some recipes may vary. We've included pressure cooking time charts as a guide (pages 248–251), but these are approximate times, and numerous variables may cause your results to be different. For example, the freshness of dried beans affects their cooking time (older beans take longer to cook), as does what they are cooked with—hard water (water that is high in mineral content), acidic ingredients, sugar and salt levels can also affect cooking times. So be flexible and experiment with what works best for you—you can always check the doneness of your food and add more time.

- Set reasonable expectations, i.e., don't expect everything you cook in the Instant Pot to be ready in a few minutes. Even though it reduces many conventional cooking times dramatically, nothing is literally "instant"—it will always take time to get up to pressure, and then to release it. (These machines are fast but not magical!)

BREAKFAST & BRUNCH

French Toast Casserole

Makes 6 servings

1 loaf (14 to 16 ounces) day-old cinnamon swirl bread*

4 ounces cream cheese, cubed

1½ cups whole milk

4 eggs

¼ cup maple syrup, plus additional for serving

⅛ teaspoon salt

1 cup water

Day-old bread is drier than fresh bread and better able to absorb the custard mixture in casseroles and bread puddings. If you only have fresh bread, bake the bread cubes on a baking sheet in a 350°F oven about 7 minutes or until lightly toasted.

1 Spray 1½ quart (6- to 7-inch) soufflé dish with nonstick cooking spray. Cut bread into 1-inch pieces. (You should have 5 to 6 cups bread cubes.) Place one third of bread in prepared soufflé dish; top with half of cream cheese cubes. Repeat layers; top with remaining bread.

2 Whisk milk, eggs, ¼ cup maple syrup and salt in medium bowl until well blended. Pour over bread and cream cheese; press gently into liquid. Cover dish with foil; let stand 30 minutes.

3 Pour water into Instant Pot; place rack in pot. Place soufflé dish on rack. Secure lid and move pressure release valve to Sealing position. Press Pressure Cook or Manual; cook at high pressure 35 minutes.

4 When cooking is complete, use natural release for 5 minutes, then release remaining pressure. Remove soufflé dish from pot. Uncover; let stand 5 minutes before serving. Cut into wedges; serve warm with additional maple syrup.

Lemon Blueberry Oatmeal

Makes 4 servings

2 tablespoons butter

1¼ cups steel-cut oats

3¾ cups water

½ teaspoon salt

2 lemons

4 tablespoons honey, divided

¾ cup fresh blueberries

½ cup chopped toasted almonds*

To toast almonds, cook in small skillet over medium heat about 5 minutes or until lightly browned and fragrant, stirring frequently.

1 Press Sauté; melt butter in Instant Pot. Add oats; cook about 6 minutes or until oats are browned and fragrant, stirring frequently. Stir in water and salt; mix well.

2 Secure lid and move pressure release valve to Sealing position. Press Pressure Cook or Manual; cook at high pressure 12 minutes.

3 Grate 4 teaspoons peel from lemons; squeeze 3 tablespoons juice.

4 When cooking is complete, use natural release for 10 minutes, then release remaining pressure. Stir oats until smooth. Add lemon juice, 2 teaspoons grated peel and 2 tablespoons honey; mix well.

5 Top each serving with blueberries, almonds and remaining lemon peel; drizzle with remaining honey.

Sticky Cinnamon Monkey Bread

Makes 6 to 8 servings

⅓ cup sugar

1 tablespoon ground cinnamon

1 container (about 16 ounces) refrigerated jumbo biscuits (8 biscuits)

¼ cup (½ stick) butter, melted

1 cup water

1 Spray 6-cup bundt pan with nonstick cooking spray. Combine sugar and cinnamon in medium bowl; mix well. Sprinkle 1 tablespoon cinnamon-sugar in bottom of prepared pan.

2 Separate biscuits; cut each biscuit into quarters. Dip each biscuit piece in butter; roll in cinnamon-sugar to coat. Layer biscuit pieces in prepared pan. Cover pan with foil.

3 Pour water into Instant Pot; place rack in pot. Place pan on rack. Secure lid and move pressure release valve to Sealing position. Press Pressure Cook or Manual; cook at high pressure 25 minutes.

4 When cooking is complete, use natural release for 10 minutes, then release remaining pressure. Remove pan from pot. Uncover; let stand 10 minutes. Invert monkey bread onto plate; serve warm.

Crustless Spinach Quiche

Makes 6 servings

6 eggs

¾ cup half-and-half

¾ teaspoon Italian seasoning

½ teaspoon salt

½ teaspoon black pepper

1 package (10 ounces) frozen chopped spinach, thawed and squeezed dry

1 cup (4 ounces) shredded Italian cheese blend

1½ cups water

1 Spray 7-inch metal cake pan with nonstick cooking spray. Beat eggs, half-and-half, Italian seasoning, salt and pepper in medium bowl until well blended. Stir in spinach and cheese; mix well. Pour into prepared pan; cover with foil.

2 Pour water into Instant Pot; place rack in pot. Place pan on rack. Secure lid and move pressure release valve to Sealing position. Press Pressure Cook or Manual; cook at high pressure 28 minutes.

3 When cooking is complete, use natural release for 5 minutes, then release remaining pressure. Remove pan from pot. Uncover; let stand 5 minutes before serving.

Tip

To remove quiche from pan for serving, run knife around edge of pan to loosen. Invert quiche onto plate; invert again onto second plate. Cut into wedges to serve.

Fruity Whole-Grain Cereal

Makes 4 to 6 servings

2¼ cups water

¼ cup steel-cut oats

¼ cup uncooked pearl barley

¼ cup uncooked brown rice

½ teaspoon salt

½ cup milk

⅓ cup golden raisins

¼ cup finely chopped dried
     dates

¼ cup chopped dried plums

2 tablespoons packed
     brown sugar

½ teaspoon ground cinnamon

1 Combine water, oats, barley, rice and salt in Instant Pot; mix well.

2 Secure lid and move pressure release valve to Sealing position. Press Pressure Cook or Manual; cook at high pressure 20 minutes.

3 When cooking is complete, use natural release for 10 minutes, then release remaining pressure.

4 Stir in milk, raisins, dates, dried plums, brown sugar and cinnamon; mix well. Serve hot. Refrigerate any leftover cereal in airtight container.

Tip

To reheat cereal, place one serving in microwavable bowl. Microwave on HIGH 30 seconds; stir. Add water or milk to reach desired consistency. Microwave just until hot.

Shakshuka

Makes 4 servings

  2 tablespoons extra virgin
       olive oil
  1 large red bell pepper,
       chopped
  1 medium onion, chopped
  3 cloves garlic, minced
  2 teaspoons sugar
  2 teaspoons ground cumin
  1 teaspoon paprika
  1 teaspoon chili powder
 ½ teaspoon salt
 ¼ teaspoon red pepper flakes
  1 can (28 ounces) crushed
       tomatoes
 ¾ cup (3 ounces) crumbled
       feta cheese
  4 eggs

1 Press Sauté; heat oil in Instant Pot. Add bell pepper and onion; cook and stir 3 minutes or until vegetables are softened. Add garlic, sugar, cumin, paprika, chili powder, salt and red pepper flakes; cook and stir 1 minute. Stir in tomatoes; mix well.

2 Secure lid and move pressure release valve to Sealing position. Press Pressure Cook or Manual; cook at high pressure 10 minutes.

3 When cooking is complete, use quick release. Stir in cheese. Make four wells in sauce for eggs, leaving space between each. Slide eggs, one at a time, into wells in sauce. (For best results, crack each egg into small bowl before sliding into sauce.)

4 Secure lid and move pressure release valve to Sealing position. Press Pressure Cook or Manual; cook at low pressure 1 minute. When cooking is complete, use quick release. To cook eggs longer, press Sauté and cook until desired doneness.

Pancake Breakfast Casserole

Makes 6 servings

4 eggs

1 cup half-and-half

2 tablespoons sugar

¾ teaspoon ground cinnamon, plus additional for garnish

½ teaspoon vanilla

9 frozen buttermilk pancakes (4-inch diameter), cut in half

1 cup water

Maple syrup

1 Spray 1½-quart (6- to 7-inch) soufflé dish with nonstick cooking spray. Beat eggs, half-and-half, sugar, ¾ teaspoon cinnamon and vanilla in medium bowl until well blended.

2 Arrange 4 or 5 pancake halves standing up around side of prepared dish. Stack remaining pancake halves in soufflé dish, making layers as even as possible. Pour egg mixture over pancakes; press pancakes gently into liquid. Cover dish with foil; refrigerate overnight.

3 Remove soufflé dish from refrigerator at least 30 minutes before cooking. Pour water into Instant Pot; place rack in pot. Place soufflé dish on rack.

4 Secure lid and move pressure release valve to Sealing position. Press Pressure Cook or Manual; cook at high pressure 30 minutes.

5 When cooking is complete, use natural release for 5 minutes, then release remaining pressure. Remove soufflé dish from pot. Uncover; sprinkle with additional cinnamon, if desired. Cut into wedges; serve warm with maple syrup.

Kale and Roasted Pepper Frittata

Makes 6 servings

10 eggs

½ cup whole milk

1 teaspoon Greek seasoning

2 cups baby kale*

1 cup (4 ounces) crumbled feta cheese with sun-dried tomatoes and basil

¾ cup diced roasted red peppers

1½ cups water

Or substitute 2 cups baby arugula or baby spinach.

1 Spray 1½-quart (6- to 7-inch) soufflé dish with nonstick cooking spray. Beat eggs, milk and Greek seasoning in medium bowl until well blended. Stir in kale, cheese and roasted peppers. Pour into prepared soufflé dish; cover with foil.

2 Pour water into Instant Pot; place rack in pot. Place soufflé dish on rack. Secure lid and move pressure release valve to Sealing position. Press Pressure Cook or Manual; cook at high pressure 30 minutes.

3 When cooking is complete, use natural release for 10 minutes, then release remaining pressure. Remove soufflé dish from pot. Uncover; let stand 5 minutes before serving.

Apple-Cinnamon Breakfast Risotto

Makes 6 servings

- 4 tablespoons (½ stick) butter, divided
- 4 medium Granny Smith apples (about 1½ pounds), peeled and diced
- 1½ teaspoons ground cinnamon, divided
- 1½ cups uncooked arborio rice
- 1 teaspoon salt
- ¼ teaspoon ground allspice
- 4 cups apple juice
- 2 tablespoons packed dark brown sugar, plus additional for serving
- 1 teaspoon vanilla
- Milk, sliced almonds and dried cranberries (optional)

1 Press Sauté; melt 2 tablespoons butter in Instant Pot. Add apples and ½ teaspoon cinnamon; cook and stir about 5 minutes or until apples are softened. Transfer to small bowl; set aside.

2 Melt remaining 2 tablespoons butter in pot. Add rice, remaining 1 teaspoon cinnamon, salt and allspice; cook and stir 1 minute. Stir in apple juice, 2 tablespoons brown sugar and vanilla; mix well.

3 Secure lid and move pressure release valve to Sealing position. Press Pressure Cook or Manual; cook at high pressure 6 minutes.

4 When cooking is complete, use quick release. Press Sauté; add reserved apples to pot. Cook and stir 1 minute or until risotto reaches desired consistency. Serve with milk, almonds, cranberries and additional brown sugar, if desired.

Parmesan Garlic Monkey Bread

Makes 6 to 8 servings

2 tablespoons butter, melted

2 tablespoons olive oil

2 cloves garlic, minced

1 teaspoon Italian seasoning

¼ teaspoon salt

1 cup grated Parmesan cheese (do not use shredded)

1 container (about 16 ounces) refrigerated jumbo biscuits (8 biscuits)

1 cup water

Pizza sauce or marinara sauce, heated (optional)

1 Spray 6-cup bundt pan with nonstick cooking spray. Combine butter, oil, garlic, Italian seasoning and salt in medium bowl; mix well. Place cheese in shallow dish.

2 Separate biscuits; cut each biscuit into quarters. Dip each biscuit piece in butter mixture; roll in cheese to coat. Layer biscuit pieces in prepared pan. Cover pan with foil.

3 Pour water into Instant Pot; place rack in pot. Place pan on rack. Secure lid and move pressure release valve to Sealing position. Press Pressure Cook or Manual; cook at high pressure 25 minutes. Preheat oven to 400°F. Line small baking sheet with foil; spray with cooking spray.

4 When cooking is complete, use natural release for 10 minutes, then release remaining pressure. Remove pan from pot. Uncover; let stand 10 minutes.

5 Invert monkey bread onto prepared baking sheet. Bake about 10 minutes or until top is golden brown. Serve with pizza sauce for dipping, if desired.

Mini Broccoli Frittatas

Makes 5 servings

1 broccoli crown
   (about 8 ounces)

1 tablespoon olive oil

⅓ cup chopped red onion

1 cup plus 2 tablespoons
   water, divided

¾ teaspoon salt, divided

¼ cup diced roasted red
   pepper (¼-inch pieces)

   Pinch red pepper flakes

½ cup (2 ounces) crumbled
   goat cheese

7 eggs

3 tablespoons grated
   Parmesan or Asiago
   cheese

3 tablespoons chopped
   fresh basil *or* ¾ teaspoon
   dried basil

2 tablespoons milk or water

¼ teaspoon black pepper

1 Spray five 6-ounce ramekins or custard cups with nonstick cooking spray. Peel off tough outer skin of broccoli stem with paring knife; chop stem into ¼-inch pieces. Chop top of broccoli into small florets (about ½ inch).

2 Press Sauté; heat oil in Instant Pot. Add onion; cook and stir 2 minutes. Add broccoli, 2 tablespoons water and ¼ teaspoon salt; cook and stir about 5 minutes or until broccoli is crisp-tender. Add roasted pepper and red pepper flakes; cook and stir 1 minute. Remove vegetables to small bowl; stir in goat cheese. Wipe out pot with paper towel.

3 Whisk eggs, Parmesan, basil, milk, remaining ½ teaspoon salt and pepper in medium bowl until well blended. Divide vegetable mixture evenly among prepared ramekins; pour egg mixture over vegetables.

4 Pour remaining 1 cup water into pot; place rack in pot. Arrange ramekins on rack, stacking as necessary. Secure lid and move pressure release valve to Sealing position. Press Pressure Cook or Manual; cook at high pressure 17 minutes.

5 When cooking is complete, use quick release. Remove ramekins from pot; cool on wire rack 5 minutes. Run small knife around edges to loosen frittatas; turn out onto plates. Serve warm.

Big Denver Omelet
Makes 6 to 8 servings

1 tablespoon butter

⅓ cup chopped onion

⅓ cup diced red bell pepper
   (¼-inch pieces)

⅓ cup diced green bell pepper
   (¼-inch pieces)

⅓ cup diced ham
   (¼-inch pieces)

8 eggs

2 tablespoons milk

½ teaspoon salt

¼ teaspoon black pepper

½ cup (2 ounces) shredded
   Cheddar cheese

1½ cups water

1 Press Sauté; melt butter in Instant Pot. Add onion, bell peppers and ham; cook and stir about 3 minutes or until vegetables begin to soften. Remove to plate to cool slightly. Wipe out pot with paper towel.

2 Spray 6-cup nonstick bundt pan generously with nonstick cooking spray. (Make sure crevices and bottom of pan are very well greased to prevent sticking.) Whisk eggs, milk, salt and black pepper in medium bowl until well blended. Stir in cheese and vegetable mixture; mix well. Pour into prepared pan; cover with foil.

3 Pour water into pot; place rack in pot. Place pan on rack. Secure lid and move pressure release valve to Sealing position. Press Pressure Cook or Manual; cook at high pressure 14 minutes.

4 When cooking is complete, use natural release for 5 minutes, then release remaining pressure. Remove pan from pot; carefully remove foil. If there is some condensation on top of omelet, blot with paper towel. Cool in pan on wire rack 10 minutes. Make sure edges and bottom of omelet are loosened before inverting omelet onto plate. Invert again onto serving plate (so more attractive side faces up). Serve warm.

Superfood Breakfast Porridge

Makes 4 servings

¾ cup steel-cut oats

¼ cup uncooked quinoa, rinsed and drained

¼ cup dried cranberries, plus additional for serving

¼ cup raisins

3 tablespoons ground flax seeds

2 tablespoons chia seeds

1 teaspoon olive oil

¼ teaspoon salt

¼ teaspoon ground cinnamon

2½ cups almond milk, plus additional for serving

1½ cups water

Maple syrup (optional)

¼ cup sliced almonds, toasted* (optional)

To toast almonds, cook and stir in small skillet over medium heat 1 to 2 minutes or until lightly browned.

1 Spray heatproof bowl (metal, glass or ceramic) that fits inside of Instant Pot with nonstick cooking spray. Combine oats, quinoa, ¼ cup cranberries, raisins, flax seeds, chia seeds, oil, salt and cinnamon in prepared bowl; mix well. Stir in 2½ cups almond milk until blended.

2 Pour water into pot; place rack in pot. Place bowl on rack. Secure lid and move pressure release valve to Sealing position. Press Pressure Cook or Manual; cook at high pressure 13 minutes.

3 When cooking is complete, use natural release. Remove bowl from pot. Stir porridge until smooth. Serve with additional almond milk, cranberries, maple syrup and almonds, if desired.

SOUPS & STEWS

One-Pot Chinese Chicken Soup
Makes 4 servings

- 1 container (32 ounces) chicken broth
- 1/3 cup reduced-sodium soy sauce
- 1 pound boneless skinless chicken thighs
- 1 package (16 ounces) frozen stir-fry vegetables (do not thaw)
- 6 ounces uncooked dried thin Chinese egg noodles
- 1 to 3 tablespoons sriracha sauce

1 Combine broth and soy sauce in Instant Pot; mix well. Add chicken. Secure lid and move pressure release valve to Sealing position. Press Pressure Cook or Manual; cook at high pressure 8 minutes.

2 When cooking is complete, use quick release. Remove chicken to bowl; set aside 5 minutes or until cool enough to handle. Shred chicken into bite-size pieces.

3 Press Sauté; add vegetables and noodles to broth mixture in pot. Cook about 3 minutes or until noodles are tender. Stir in chicken and 1 tablespoon sriracha sauce; taste and add additional sauce for a spicier flavor.

Savory Cod Stew
Makes 6 to 8 servings

8 ounces bacon, chopped

1 large onion, diced

1 large carrot, diced

2 stalks celery, diced

2 cloves garlic, minced

1 can (28 ounces) plum tomatoes, undrained, coarsely chopped

2 potatoes, peeled and diced

1 cup clam juice

3 tablespoons tomato paste

3 tablespoons chopped fresh Italian parsley

½ teaspoon salt

¼ teaspoon black pepper

3 saffron threads

2½ pounds fresh cod, skin removed, cut into 1½-inch pieces

1 Press Sauté; cook bacon in Instant Pot until crisp. Drain off all but 2 tablespoons drippings.

2 Add onion, carrot, celery and garlic to pot; cook and stir 5 minutes or until vegetables are softened. Add tomatoes with juice, potatoes, clam juice, tomato paste, parsley, salt, pepper and saffron; cook and stir 2 minutes.

3 Secure lid and move pressure release valve to Sealing position. Press Pressure Cook or Manual; cook at high pressure 2 minutes.

4 When cooking is complete, use quick release. Add cod to pot. Secure lid and move pressure release valve to Sealing position. Press Pressure Cook or Manual; cook at low pressure 1 minute.

5 When cooking is complete, use quick release.

Mushroom Barley Soup
Makes 6 to 8 servings

2 tablespoons olive oil

1 onion, chopped

2 carrots, chopped

2 stalks celery, chopped

3 cloves garlic, minced

1 teaspoon salt

½ teaspoon dried thyme

½ teaspoon black pepper

5 cups vegetable or
   chicken broth

1 package (16 ounces)
   sliced mushrooms

½ cup uncooked pearl barley

½ ounce dried porcini or
   shiitake mushrooms

1 Press Sauté; heat oil in Instant Pot. Add onion, carrots and celery; cook and stir 5 minutes or until vegetables are softened. Add garlic, salt, thyme and pepper; cook and stir 1 minute. Stir in broth, sliced mushrooms, barley and dried mushrooms; mix well.

2 Secure lid and move pressure release valve to Sealing position. Press Pressure Cook or Manual; cook at high pressure 22 minutes.

3 When cooking is complete, use natural release for 10 minutes, then release remaining pressure.

Salsa Verde Chicken Stew

Makes 4 to 6 servings

2 cans (about 15 ounces each) black beans, rinsed and drained

1½ pounds boneless skinless chicken breasts, cut into 1-inch pieces

1 jar (16 ounces) salsa verde

1½ cups frozen corn

¾ cup chopped fresh cilantro

Diced avocado (optional)

1 Combine beans, chicken and salsa in Instant Pot; mix well.

2 Secure lid and move pressure release valve to Sealing position. Press Pressure Cook or Manual; cook at high pressure 4 minutes.

3 When cooking is complete, use quick release. Press Sauté; add corn to pot. Cook about 3 minutes or until heated through. Stir in cilantro; mix well. Garnish with avocado.

Tuscan Bread Soup

Makes 6 to 8 servings

2 tablespoons olive oil

1 onion, cut in half and thinly sliced

2 stalks celery, diced

1 large carrot, julienned

3 cloves garlic, minced

1½ teaspoons salt

1 teaspoon Italian seasoning

1 bay leaf

¼ teaspoon black pepper

¼ teaspoon red pepper flakes (optional)

4 cups vegetable broth

1 can (28 ounces) whole tomatoes, undrained, coarsely chopped

1 can (about 15 ounces) cannellini beans, rinsed and drained

1 bunch kale, stemmed and coarsely chopped *or* 3 cups thinly sliced cabbage

8 ounces rustic Italian bread, cubed (½-inch pieces)

2 medium zucchini, thinly sliced (⅛-inch slices)

1 medium yellow squash, thinly sliced (⅛-inch slices)

Shredded Parmesan cheese (optional)

1 Press Sauté; heat oil in Instant Pot. Add onion, celery and carrot; cook and stir 5 minutes. Add garlic, salt, Italian seasoning, bay leaf, black pepper and red pepper flakes, if desired; cook and stir 1 minute. Stir in broth, tomatoes with juice and beans; mix well.

2 Secure lid and move pressure release valve to Sealing position. Press Pressure Cook or Manual; cook at high pressure 8 minutes. When cooking is complete, use quick release.

3 Add kale, bread, zucchini and yellow squash to pot. Secure lid and move pressure release valve to Sealing position. Press Pressure Cook or Manual; cook at high pressure 1 minute.

4 When cooking is complete, use quick release. Serve with cheese, if desired.

Note

This is a great recipe to use a spiralizer if you have one. Use the spiral slicing blade to spiral the zucchini and yellow squash, then cut in half to make half moon slices. Use the thin ribbon blade to spiral the onion and carrot, and then cut into desired lengths.

Persian Green Stew

Makes 6 servings

1½ pounds boneless leg of lamb or shoulder, cut into 1-inch cubes

1 teaspoon ground turmeric

¾ teaspoon salt, divided

½ teaspoon curry powder

½ teaspoon ground black pepper, divided

2 tablespoons olive oil, divided

2 medium onions, chopped

1 package (about 5 ounces) baby spinach, chopped

2 cups chopped fresh Italian parsley

6 green onions, chopped

1 cup chopped fresh cilantro

1 can (about 15 ounces) cannellini beans, rinsed and drained

½ cup beef broth

2 tablespoons lime juice

Hot cooked basmati rice

1 Combine lamb, turmeric, ½ teaspoon salt, curry powder and ¼ teaspoon pepper in large bowl; toss to coat. Press Sauté; heat 1 tablespoon oil in Instant Pot. Cook lamb in two batches about 4 minutes or until browned, stirring occasionally. Remove to plate.

2 Add remaining 1 tablespoon oil, onions and remaining ¼ teaspoon salt to pot; adjust heat to low. Cook 5 to 7 minutes or until onions begin to brown, stirring occasionally. Add spinach, parsley, green onions and cilantro; cook 3 minutes or until spinach is wilted, scraping up browned bits from bottom of pot. Stir in lamb, beans and broth; mix well.

3 Secure lid and move pressure release valve to Sealing position. Press Pressure Cook or Manual; cook at high pressure 20 minutes.

4 When cooking is complete, use natural release for 10 minutes, then release remaining pressure. Press Sauté; stir in lime juice and remaining ¼ teaspoon pepper. Cook about 3 minutes or until liquid is reduced slightly. Serve over rice.

Creamy Tomato Soup

Makes 6 servings

2 tablespoons olive oil

2 tablespoons butter

1 large onion, finely chopped

2 cloves garlic, minced

2 teaspoons sugar

1½ teaspoons salt

½ teaspoon dried oregano

2 cans (28 ounces each) peeled Italian plum tomatoes, undrained

Focaccia Croutons (recipe follows, optional)

½ cup whipping cream

1 Press Sauté; heat oil and butter in Instant Pot. Add onion; cook and stir 5 minutes or until softened. Add garlic, sugar, salt and oregano; cook and stir 30 seconds. Stir in tomatoes with juice; mix well.

2 Secure lid and move pressure release valve to Sealing position. Press Pressure Cook or Manual; cook at high pressure 8 minutes. Prepare Focaccia Croutons, if desired.

3 When cooking is complete, use natural release for 10 minutes, then release remaining pressure.

4 Use hand-held immersion blender to blend soup until smooth. Stir in cream until well blended. Serve soup with croutons.

Focaccia Croutons

Combine 4 cups ½-inch focaccia cubes (half of 9-ounce loaf), 1 tablespoon olive oil and ½ teaspoon black pepper in large bowl; toss to coat. Spread on large baking sheet; bake in preheated 350°F oven about 10 minutes or until golden brown.

Quick Shrimp and Okra Stew

Makes 4 servings

1 teaspoon vegetable oil

½ cup finely chopped onion

8 ounces okra, ends trimmed, cut into ½-inch slices

1 can (about 14 ounces) whole tomatoes, undrained, chopped

1 teaspoon dried thyme

¾ teaspoon salt

8 ounces medium raw shrimp, peeled and deveined

¾ cup fresh corn or thawed frozen corn

½ teaspoon hot pepper sauce

1 Press Sauté; heat oil in Instant Pot. Add onion; cook and stir 3 minutes or until softened. Add okra; cook and stir 3 minutes. Add tomatoes with juice, thyme and salt; mix well.

2 Secure lid and move pressure release valve to Sealing position. Press Pressure Cook or Manual; cook at high pressure 4 minutes.

3 When cooking is complete, use quick release.

4 Press Sauté; add shrimp, corn and hot pepper sauce to pot. Cook 3 minutes or until shrimp turn pink and opaque, stirring frequently.

Coconut Curry Chicken Soup

Makes 4 servings

1 can (about 14 ounces) coconut milk, divided

1½ cups chicken broth

1 cup chopped onion

2 tablespoons curry powder

1 teaspoon salt

½ teaspoon ground ginger

⅛ teaspoon ground red pepper

1½ pounds boneless skinless chicken thighs

¼ cup chopped fresh cilantro or mint

3 cups cooked rice (optional)

Lime wedges (optional)

1 Shake or stir coconut milk until well blended and smooth. Combine half of coconut milk, broth, onion, curry powder, salt, ginger and red pepper in Instant Pot; mix well. Add chicken, pressing into liquid.

2 Secure lid and move pressure release valve to Sealing position. Press Pressure Cook or Manual; cook at high pressure 9 minutes.

3 When cooking is complete, use natural release for 10 minutes, then release remaining pressure. Remove chicken to plate; let stand until cool enough to handle.

4 Shred chicken into bite-size pieces. Press Sauté; add to pot with remaining coconut milk and cilantro. Cook 3 minutes or until heated through, stirring occasionally. Spoon rice over each serving, if desired; garnish with lime wedges.

West African Peanut Soup

Makes 6 to 8 servings

2 tablespoons vegetable oil

1 large onion, chopped

½ cup chopped roasted peanuts

1½ tablespoons minced fresh ginger

4 cloves garlic, minced (about 1 tablespoon)

1 teaspoon salt

3 cups vegetable broth

⅓ cup unsweetened peanut butter (creamy or chunky)

2 sweet potatoes, peeled and cut into ½-inch cubes

1 can (28 ounces) whole tomatoes, drained and coarsely chopped

1 bunch kale or Swiss chard, stemmed and shredded

¼ teaspoon ground red pepper

1 Press Sauté; heat oil in Instant Pot. Add onion; cook and stir 5 minutes or until softened. Add peanuts, ginger, garlic and salt; cook and stir 1 minute. Stir in broth and peanut butter until blended. Add sweet potatoes, tomatoes, kale and red pepper; mix well.

2 Secure lid and move pressure release valve to Sealing position. Press Pressure Cook or Manual; cook at high pressure 3 minutes.

3 When cooking is complete, use quick release.

Lamb and Chickpea Stew

Makes 4 to 6 servings

1 cup dried chickpeas, soaked 8 hours or overnight

2 tablespoons vegetable oil, divided

1 pound lamb stew meat

1 large onion, chopped

1 tablespoon minced garlic

1½ teaspoons salt

1½ teaspoons ground cumin

1 teaspoon ground turmeric

1 teaspoon ground coriander

1 teaspoon ground cinnamon

¼ teaspoon black pepper

1 can (about 14 ounces) diced tomatoes

1½ cups chicken broth

½ cup chopped dried apricots, divided

¼ cup chopped fresh Italian parsley

2 tablespoons lemon juice

1 tablespoon honey

Hot cooked couscous

1 Drain and rinse chickpeas. Press Sauté; heat 1 tablespoon oil in Instant Pot. Add lamb; cook 6 minutes or until browned, stirring occasionally. Add remaining 1 tablespoon oil and onion to pot; cook and stir 3 minutes or until softened. Add garlic, salt, cumin, turmeric, coriander, cinnamon and pepper; cook and stir 1 minute. Add tomatoes and broth; cook and stir 2 minutes, scraping up browned bits from bottom of pot. Stir in chickpeas and ¼ cup apricots; mix well.

2 Secure lid and move pressure release valve to Sealing position. Press Pressure Cook or Manual; cook at high pressure 20 minutes.

3 When cooking is complete, use natural release for 10 minutes, then release remaining pressure.

4 Press Sauté; add remaining ¼ cup apricots to pot. Cook 5 minutes or until sauce is reduced and thickens slightly, stirring frequently. Stir in parsley, lemon juice and honey. Serve with couscous.

Pork and Cabbage Soup

Makes 6 servings

8 ounces pork loin, cut into ½-inch pieces

1 medium onion, chopped

2 slices bacon, finely chopped

1 can (about 28 ounces) whole tomatoes, undrained, coarsely chopped

1 teaspoon salt

1 bay leaf

¾ teaspoon dried marjoram

⅛ teaspoon black pepper

¼ medium cabbage, chopped, divided (about 5 cups)

2 medium carrots, cut into ½-inch slices

1 cup chicken broth

2 tablespoons chopped fresh parsley

1 Press Sauté; add pork, onion and bacon to Instant Pot. Cook and stir about 5 minutes until pork is no longer pink and onion is softened. Add tomatoes with liquid, salt, bay leaf, marjoram and pepper; cook 2 minutes, scraping up browned bits from bottom of pot. Stir in half of cabbage, carrots and broth; mix well.

2 Secure lid and move pressure release valve to Sealing position. Press Pressure Cook or Manual; cook at high pressure 8 minutes.

3 When cooking is complete, use natural release for 10 minutes, then release remaining pressure. Remove and discard bay leaf.

4 Press Sauté; add remaining half of cabbage to pot. Cook about 3 minutes or until cabbage is wilted, stirring frequently. Stir in parsley.

Sausage and Potato Soup

Makes 4 to 6 servings

1 tablespoon olive oil

8 ounces kielbasa sausage, halved lengthwise, then cut crosswise into ½-inch slices

1 medium onion, diced

1 teaspoon dried oregano

1 teaspoon ground cumin

1 tablespoon tomato paste

1 large baking potato, peeled and cut into ½-inch cubes

1 can (about 15 ounces) dark red kidney beans, rinsed and drained

1 can (about 14 ounces) diced tomatoes

1 cup beef broth

1 medium green bell pepper, diced

¼ teaspoon salt

1 Press Sauté; heat oil in Instant Pot. Add sausage and onion; cook 5 minutes or until sausage is lightly browned. Add oregano and cumin; cook and stir 30 seconds. Add tomato paste; cook and stir 1 minute. Stir in potato, beans, tomatoes, broth, bell pepper and salt; mix well.

2 Secure lid and move pressure release valve to Sealing position. Press Pressure Cook or Manual; cook at high pressure 3 minutes.

3 When cooking is complete, use natural release for 10 minutes, then release remaining pressure.

Curried Chicken and Winter Vegetable Stew

Makes 4 to 6 servings

1 tablespoon vegetable oil

1 medium onion, chopped

1 tablespoon curry powder

1 clove garlic, minced

1 pound boneless skinless chicken breasts, cut into ½-inch pieces

1 can (about 14 ounces) diced tomatoes

1 cup chicken broth

2 medium turnips, cut into 1-inch pieces

2 medium carrots, cut into 1-inch slices

½ cup raisins (optional)

¼ cup tomato paste

1 teaspoon salt

⅛ teaspoon ground red pepper

1 Press Sauté; adjust heat to low. Heat oil in Instant Pot. Add onion; cook and stir 3 minutes or until softened. Add curry powder and garlic; cook and stir 1 minute. Stir in chicken, tomatoes, broth, turnips, carrots, raisins, if desired, tomato paste, salt and red pepper; mix well.

2 Secure lid and move pressure release valve to Sealing position. Press Pressure Cook or Manual; cook at high pressure 5 minutes.

3 When cooking is complete, use natural release for 5 minutes, then release remaining pressure.

Serving Suggestion

Serve with hot cooked couscous or brown rice.

Beef, Lentil and Onion Soup

Makes 4 servings

1 tablespoon olive oil

12 ounces beef stew meat

2 cups chopped carrots

1 medium onion, chopped

1 cup sliced celery

1 cup dried lentils, rinsed and sorted

2 teaspoons dried thyme

¼ teaspoon salt

¼ teaspoon black pepper

3¼ cups water

1 can (about 10 ounces) condensed French onion soup, undiluted

1 Press Sauté; heat oil in Instant Pot. Add beef; cook 5 to 7 minutes or until browned, stirring occasionally. Stir in carrots, onion, celery, lentils, thyme, salt and pepper. Add water and soup; mix well.

2 Secure lid and move pressure release valve to Sealing position. Press Pressure Cook or Manual; cook at high pressure 20 minutes.

3 When cooking is complete, use natural release for 10 minutes, then release remaining pressure.

Turkey Vegetable Rice Soup
Makes 6 to 8 servings

6 cups cold water

2 pounds turkey drumsticks (3 small)

1 large onion, cut into 8 wedges

4 tablespoons soy sauce, divided

1 bay leaf

½ teaspoon salt, divided

½ teaspoon black pepper, divided

2 carrots, sliced

8 ounces mushrooms, sliced

2 cups coarsely chopped bok choy (about 6 ounces)

½ cup uncooked rice

1½ cups fresh snow peas, cut in half crosswise

Sriracha or hot pepper sauce (optional)

1 Combine water, turkey, onion, 2 tablespoons soy sauce, bay leaf, ¼ teaspoon salt and ¼ teaspoon pepper in Instant Pot.

2 Secure lid and move pressure release valve to Sealing position. Press Pressure Cook or Manual; cook at high pressure 25 minutes.

3 When cooking is complete, use natural release for 10 minutes, then release remaining pressure. Remove turkey to plate; let stand until cool enough to handle.

4 Meanwhile, add carrots, mushrooms, bok choy, rice and remaining ¼ teaspoon salt to pot; mix well. Secure lid and move pressure release valve to Sealing position. Press Pressure Cook or Manual; cook at high pressure 4 minutes. When cooking is complete, use natural release for 5 minutes, then release remaining pressure. Remove and discard bay leaf.

5 Remove turkey meat from bones; discard skin and bones. Cut turkey into bite-size pieces. Press Sauté; add turkey, snow peas, remaining 2 tablespoons soy sauce and ¼ teaspoon pepper to pot. Cook and stir 2 to 3 minutes or until snow peas are crisp-tender, stirring occasionally. Serve with sriracha sauce, if desired.

Spicy-Sweet Lamb Tagine
Makes 4 to 6 servings

¾ cup dried chickpeas, soaked 8 hours or overnight

1 tablespoon olive oil

2 pounds boneless lamb shoulder or leg, cut into 1½-inch pieces

3 medium onions, each cut into 8 wedges

3 cloves garlic, minced

2 teaspoons ground ginger

2 teaspoons ground cinnamon

1 teaspoon black pepper

1½ cups water

1 can (about 14 ounces) diced tomatoes

2 teaspoons salt

1 small butternut squash, peeled and cut into 1-inch pieces (about 3 cups)

1 cup chopped pitted prunes

2 medium zucchini, halved lengthwise and cut crosswise into ½-inch slices

Hot cooked couscous (optional)

¼ cup chopped fresh cilantro or parsley

1 Drain and rinse chickpeas. Press Sauté; heat oil in Instant Pot. Add lamb in two batches; cook about 5 minutes or until browned. Remove to plate.

2 Add onions, garlic, ginger, cinnamon and pepper to pot; cook and stir 30 seconds or until spices are fragrant. Add water; cook 2 minutes, scraping up browned bits from bottom of pot. Stir in tomatoes, chickpeas and salt; mix well. Return lamb to pot.

3 Secure lid and move pressure release valve to Sealing position. Press Pressure Cook or Manual; cook at high pressure 15 minutes. When cooking is complete, use quick release.

4 Add butternut squash and prunes to pot. Secure lid and move pressure release valve to Sealing position. Press Pressure Cook or Manual; cook at high pressure 3 minutes. When cooking is complete, use quick release.

5 Press Sauté; add zucchini to pot. Cook 4 minutes or until zucchini is crisp-tender, stirring occasionally. Serve stew over couscous, if desired. Sprinkle with cilantro.

Thai Pumpkin Chicken Soup

Makes 6 servings

1 tablespoon vegetable oil

1 pound boneless skinless chicken breasts, cut into 1-inch pieces

1 white onion, thinly sliced

2 stalks celery, diced

2 carrots, diced

1 tablespoon minced garlic

1 tablespoon minced fresh ginger

½ teaspoon salt

¼ to ½ teaspoon red pepper flakes

2 cups chicken broth

1 cup canned pumpkin

½ cup creamy peanut butter

½ cup minced fresh cilantro, divided

2 tablespoons rice vinegar

1 tablespoon cornstarch

2 tablespoons lime juice

Hot cooked jasmine or basmati rice

2 green onions, minced

½ cup roasted unsalted peanuts, coarsely chopped

Lime wedges (optional)

1 Press Sauté; heat oil in Instant Pot. Add chicken; cook and stir 5 minutes or until no longer pink. Add onion, celery, carrots, garlic, ginger, salt and red pepper flakes to pot; cook and stir 5 minutes or until vegetables begin to soften. Stir in broth, pumpkin, peanut butter, ¼ cup cilantro and vinegar; mix well.

2 Secure lid and move pressure release valve to Sealing position. Press Pressure Cook or Manual; cook at high pressure 5 minutes.

3 When cooking is complete, use natural release for 10 minutes, then release remaining pressure.

4 Stir ¼ cup hot soup into cornstarch in small bowl until smooth. Press Sauté; add cornstarch mixture to pot. Cook and stir 2 to 3 minutes or until soup thickens. Stir in lime juice. Serve soup with rice, remaining ¼ cup cilantro, green onions, peanuts and lime wedges, if desired.

Split Pea Soup

Makes 4 to 6 servings

8 slices bacon, chopped

1 onion, chopped

2 carrots, chopped

1 stalk celery, chopped

1 clove garlic, minced

½ teaspoon dried thyme

1 container (32 ounces) chicken broth

2 cups water

1 package (16 ounces) dried split peas, rinsed and sorted

¾ teaspoon salt

½ teaspoon black pepper

1 bay leaf

1 Press Sauté; cook bacon in Instant Pot until crisp. Remove to paper towel-lined plate. Drain off all but 1 tablespoon drippings.

2 Add onion, carrots and celery to pot; cook and stir 5 minutes or until vegetables are softened. Add garlic and thyme; cook and stir 1 minute. Stir in broth and water, scraping up browned bits from bottom of pot. Add split peas, half of bacon, salt, pepper and bay leaf; mix well.

3 Secure lid and move pressure release valve to Sealing position. Press Pressure Cook or Manual; cook at high pressure 8 minutes.

4 When cooking is complete, use natural release for 10 minutes, then release remaining pressure. Stir soup; remove and discard bay leaf. Top with remaining bacon.

Note

The soup may seem thin immediately after cooking, but it will thicken upon standing. If prepared in advance and refrigerated, thin the soup with water when reheating until it reaches the desired consistency.

CHICKEN & TURKEY

Asian Chicken and Noodles

Makes 4 servings

1 tablespoon vegetable oil

1 pound boneless skinless chicken breasts, cut into 1×½-inch pieces

1 bottle or jar (about 12 ounces) stir-fry sauce

¾ cup chicken broth or water

8 ounces uncooked thin Pad Thai rice noodles (⅛ inch wide)

1 package (16 ounces) frozen stir-fry vegetable blend (do not thaw)

1 Press Sauté; heat oil in Instant Pot. Add chicken; cook about 4 minutes or until no longer pink, stirring frequently.

2 Stir in stir-fry sauce and broth; mix well. Top with noodles, breaking to fit as necessary. Cover with vegetables in even layer. *Do not stir.*

3 Secure lid and move pressure release valve to Sealing position. Press Pressure Cook or Manual; cook at high pressure 2 minutes.

4 When cooking is complete, use quick release. Stir with tongs to separate noodles and coat noodles and vegetables with sauce. If there is excess liquid in pot, press Sauté; cook and stir 2 minutes or until liquid has evaporated.

White Chicken Chili

Makes 6 servings

1	tablespoon vegetable oil
1½	pounds boneless skinless chicken breasts
2	medium onions, chopped
1	can (4 ounces) diced green chiles
1	tablespoon minced garlic
2	teaspoons ground cumin
1	teaspoon salt
1	teaspoon dried oregano
¼	teaspoon black pepper
¼	teaspoon ground red pepper
1½	cups chicken broth
2	cans (about 15 ounces each) Great Northern beans, rinsed and drained
¼	cup chopped fresh cilantro

1 Press Sauté; heat oil in Instant Pot. Add chicken; cook about 6 minutes or until browned on both sides. Remove to plate. Add onions and chiles to pot; cook and stir 3 minutes. Add garlic, cumin, salt, oregano, black pepper and red pepper; cook and stir 1 minute. Stir in broth, scraping up browned bits from bottom of pot. Stir in beans; mix well. Return chicken to pot, pressing into liquid.

2 Secure lid and move pressure release valve to Sealing position. Press Pressure Cook or Manual; cook at high pressure 7 minutes.

3 When cooking is complete, use quick release. Remove chicken to clean plate; set aside until cool enough to handle.

4 Shred chicken into bite-size pieces; return to pot. Press Sauté; cook 2 to 3 minutes or until chili thickens slightly. Sprinkle with cilantro.

Herb Lemon Turkey Breast

Makes 4 servings

½ cup lemon juice

½ cup dry white wine

4 cloves garlic, minced

1 teaspoon salt

½ teaspoon dried parsley flakes

½ teaspoon dried tarragon

½ teaspoon dried rosemary

¼ teaspoon ground sage

¼ teaspoon black pepper

1 boneless turkey breast (about 3 pounds)

Fresh rosemary sprigs and lemon slices (optional)

1 Combine lemon juice, wine, garlic, salt, parsley flakes, tarragon, dried rosemary, sage and pepper in measuring cup or small bowl; mix well.

2 Place turkey breast in Instant Pot; pour juice mixture over turkey, turning to coat. (Turkey should be right side up for cooking.)

3 Secure lid and move pressure release valve to Sealing position. Press Pressure Cook or Manual; cook at high pressure 30 minutes.

4 When cooking is complete, use natural release for 10 minutes, then release remaining pressure. Remove turkey to cutting board; tent with foil. Let stand 10 minutes before slicing.

5 Use cooking liquid as sauce, if desired, or thicken liquid with flour (see Tip). Garnish as desired.

Tip

If desired, prepare gravy with cooking liquid after removing turkey from pot. Place ¼ cup all-purpose flour in small bowl; stir in ½ cup cooking liquid from pot until smooth. Press Sauté; add flour mixture to pot. Cook 5 minutes or until gravy thickens, stirring frequently.

Chicken and Sausage Jambalaya

Makes 6 to 8 servings

1	tablespoon vegetable oil
12	ounces andouille sausage or other smoked sausage, cut into ¼-inch slices
12	ounces boneless skinless chicken breast, cut into 1-inch pieces
1	onion, chopped
½	red bell pepper, diced
½	green bell pepper, diced
4	cloves garlic, minced
1½	tablespoons Cajun seasoning
¾	teaspoon dried thyme
1	can (about 14 ounces) diced tomatoes
1½	cups uncooked rice, rinsed well and drained
¾	cup chicken broth
2	bay leaves
	Sliced green onions and/or chopped fresh parsley (optional)

1 Press Sauté; heat oil in Instant Pot. Add sausage; cook about 5 minutes or until browned, stirring occasionally. Remove to plate.

2 Add chicken to pot; cook and stir 3 minutes or just until outside of chicken is no longer pink. Add onion, bell peppers, garlic, Cajun seasoning and thyme; cook 2 minutes, scraping up browned bits from bottom of pot.

3 Return sausage to pot; stir in tomatoes, rice, broth and bay leaves. Secure lid and move pressure release valve to Sealing position. Press Pressure Cook or Manual; cook at high pressure 7 minutes.

4 When cooking is complete, use natural release for 10 minutes, then release remaining pressure. Stir rice; remove and discard bay leaves. Sprinkle with green onions and parsley, if desired.

Greek Braised Cinnamon Chicken

Makes 4 servings

4 chicken leg quarters (drumstick and thigh, 10 to 12 ounces each)

1¾ teaspoons salt, divided

¾ teaspoon black pepper, divided

¼ plus ⅛ teaspoon ground cinnamon, divided

2 tablespoons olive oil

2 medium onions, chopped

3 cloves garlic, minced

1 can (28 ounces) whole tomatoes, undrained, coarsely chopped or crushed with hands

½ cup chicken broth

1 stick cinnamon

Chopped fresh parsley

Grated Kasseri* or Romano cheese (optional)

Kasseri is a semi-hard Greek sheep's milk cheese with a mild buttery and slightly piquant flavor.

1 Season both sides of chicken with ¾ teaspoon salt, ¼ teaspoon pepper and ⅛ teaspoon ground cinnamon. Press Sauté; heat oil in Instant Pot. Cook chicken in two batches about 5 minutes per side or until browned. Remove to plate. Drain off all but 2 tablespoons fat from pot.

2 Add onions to pot; cook and stir 3 minutes or until softened. Add garlic and remaining ¼ teaspoon ground cinnamon; cook and stir 1 minute. Stir in tomatoes, broth, cinnamon stick, remaining 1 teaspoon salt and ½ teaspoon pepper; mix well. Return chicken to pot, pressing down to partially submerge chicken in sauce.

3 Secure lid and move pressure release valve to Sealing position. Press Pressure Cook or Manual; cook at high pressure 11 minutes.

4 When cooking is complete, use natural release for 5 minutes, then release remaining pressure. Remove chicken to serving platter; tent with foil.

5 Press Sauté; cook 5 to 10 minutes or until sauce reduces and thickens slightly. Pour sauce over chicken; sprinkle with parsley and cheese, if desired.

Simple Rotisserie Chicken

Makes 4 servings

1 whole chicken (about 4 pounds)

2 tablespoons rotisserie chicken seasoning (see Tip)

1 tablespoon butter

1 tablespoon olive oil

1 cup chicken broth

Fresh parsley sprigs and lemon wedges (optional)

1 Pat chicken dry. Tie drumsticks together with kitchen string and tuck wing tips under. Sprinkle seasoning inside cavity and over all sides of chicken, pressing to adhere.

2 Press Sauté; heat butter and oil in Instant Pot. Add chicken, breast side up; cook about 5 minutes or until browned. Turn chicken over using tongs and spatula; cook about 5 minutes or until browned. Remove chicken to plate.

3 Add broth to pot; cook 1 minute, scraping up browned bits from bottom of pot. Place rack in pot; place chicken on rack, breast side up.

4 Secure lid and move pressure release valve to Sealing position. Press Pressure Cook or Manual; cook at high pressure 21 minutes.*

5 When cooking is complete, use natural release for 15 minutes, then release remaining pressure. Remove chicken to cutting board; tent with foil and let stand 10 minutes before carving. If desired, strain cooking liquid and serve with chicken. Garnish with parsley and lemon wedges.

When fully cooked, the temperature of the chicken (tested in the thigh) should be 165°F. A chicken larger than 4 pounds may take an additional 3 minutes to cook, while a smaller chicken may take a few minutes less.

Tip

Rotisserie chicken seasoning is available in the spice section of many supermarkets. If you can't find it, use a basic poultry seasoning or Italian seasoning combined with 1 teaspoon salt and 1 teaspoon paprika. Or use your favorite seasoning blend.

Chipotle BBQ Turkey Sandwiches

Makes 4 servings

1 tablespoon vegetable oil

1 small red onion, chopped

½ teaspoon chipotle chili powder

¾ cup plus 2 tablespoons barbecue sauce, divided

1 package (24 ounces) turkey tenderloins (2 tenderloins), each cut in half

4 sandwich buns

1 Press Sauté; heat oil in Instant Pot. Add onion; cook and stir 3 minutes or until softened. Add chili powder; cook and stir 30 seconds. Stir in ¾ cup barbecue sauce; mix well. Add turkey; turn to coat.

2 Secure lid and move pressure release valve to Sealing position. Press Pressure Cook or Manual; cook at high pressure 20 minutes.

3 When cooking is complete, use natural release for 10 minutes, then release remaining pressure. Remove turkey to bowl; let stand 5 minutes. Shred into bite-size pieces with tongs or two forks.

4 Meanwhile, press Sauté; adjust heat to low. Cook 5 minutes or until sauce reduces slightly. Add shredded turkey and remaining 2 tablespoons barbecue sauce to pot; cook 2 minutes, stirring frequently. Serve on buns.

Speedy Chicken Adobo

Makes 4 servings

⅓ cup cider vinegar

⅓ cup reduced-sodium
  soy sauce

5 cloves garlic, minced

3 bay leaves

1 teaspoon black pepper

2½ pounds bone-in skin-on
  chicken thighs (about 6)

  Hot cooked rice (optional)

  Sliced green onion
   (optional)

1 Combine vinegar, soy sauce, garlic, bay leaves and pepper in Instant Pot; mix well. Add chicken; turn to coat. Arrange chicken skin side down in liquid.

2 Secure lid and move pressure release valve to Sealing position. Press Pressure Cook or Manual; cook at high pressure 13 minutes. Preheat broiler. Line baking sheet with foil.

3 When cooking is complete, use natural release for 10 minutes, then release remaining pressure. Remove chicken to prepared baking sheet, skin side up.

4 Broil about 4 minutes or until skin is browned and crisp. Meanwhile, press Sauté; cook liquid in pot about 5 minutes or until sauce reduces slightly. Serve sauce over chicken and rice, if desired. Garnish with green onion.

Lemon-Mint Meatballs with Orzo

Makes 4 servings

Meatballs

- ½ cup panko bread crumbs
- 2 green onions, minced
- 2 tablespoons minced fresh mint
- 1 teaspoon salt
- 1 teaspoon grated lemon peel
- ½ teaspoon dried oregano
- ¼ teaspoon black pepper
- 1 egg
- 3 cloves garlic, minced
- 1 package (16 ounces) ground chicken

Orzo

- 3 cups chicken or vegetable broth
- 3 cloves garlic, thinly sliced
- 1 teaspoon salt
- 1 teaspoon grated lemon peel
- 2 cups uncooked orzo pasta
- 1 package (about 5 ounces) baby spinach

1 For meatballs, combine panko, green onions, mint, 1 teaspoon salt, 1 teaspoon lemon peel, oregano and pepper in medium bowl; mix well. Stir in egg and minced garlic. Add chicken; stir until well blended. Shape 2 tablespoons mixture into a ball; repeat with remaining mixture.

2 For orzo, combine broth, sliced garlic, 1 teaspoon salt and 1 teaspoon lemon peel in Instant Pot. Stir in orzo; mix well. Arrange meatballs in single layer in pot.

3 Secure lid and move pressure release valve to Sealing position. Press Pressure Cook or Manual; cook at high pressure 5 minutes.

4 When cooking is complete, use quick release. Transfer meatballs to plate. (Leave orzo in pot.) Press Sauté; add spinach to pot. Cook and stir 2 to 3 minutes or until spinach is wilted. Serve meatballs over orzo mixture.

Butter Chicken
Makes 4 to 6 servings

2 tablespoons butter

1 onion, chopped

4 cloves garlic, minced

1 teaspoon minced fresh ginger

1 teaspoon ground turmeric

1 teaspoon ground coriander

1 teaspoon garam masala

1 teaspoon ground cumin

½ teaspoon ground red pepper

½ teaspoon paprika

1 can (about 14 ounces) diced tomatoes

¾ teaspoon salt

2 pounds boneless skinless chicken breasts, cut into 2-inch pieces

½ cup whipping cream

Chopped fresh cilantro

Hot cooked rice (optional)

1 Press Sauté; melt butter in Instant Pot. Add onion; cook and stir about 4 minutes or until onion begins to turn golden. Add garlic and ginger; cook and stir 1 minute. Add turmeric, coriander, garam masala, cumin, red pepper and paprika; cook and stir 30 seconds. Add tomatoes and salt; cook and stir 2 minutes. Stir in chicken; mix well.

2 Secure lid and move pressure release valve to Sealing position. Press Pressure Cook or Manual; cook at high pressure 8 minutes.

3 When cooking is complete, use natural release for 10 minutes, then release remaining pressure.

4 Press Sauté; adjust heat to low. Stir in cream; cook 5 minutes or until heated through. Sprinkle with cilantro; serve with rice, if desired.

Turkey Stroganoff

Makes 4 servings

 1 tablespoon olive oil
 4 cups sliced mushrooms
 2 stalks celery, sliced
 2 medium shallots *or*
    ½ small onion, minced
 2 turkey tenderloins
    (about 5 ounces each),
    cut into 1-inch pieces
 ¼ cup chicken broth
 1½ tablespoons
    Worcestershire sauce
 ¾ teaspoon salt
 ½ teaspoon dried thyme
 ¼ teaspoon black pepper
 ½ cup sour cream
 1 tablespoon all-purpose
    flour
    Hot cooked egg noodles

1 Press Sauté; heat oil in Instant Pot. Add mushrooms, celery and shallots; cook and stir 5 minutes or until vegetables are softened. Add turkey, broth, Worcestershire sauce, salt, thyme and pepper; mix well.

2 Secure lid and move pressure release valve to Sealing position. Press Pressure Cook or Manual; cook at high pressure 6 minutes.

3 When cooking is complete, use natural release for 5 minutes, then release remaining pressure.

4 Combine sour cream and flour in small bowl; stir in ¼ cup hot cooking liquid from pot until smooth. Press Sauté; add sour cream mixture to pot. Cook and stir 3 minutes or until sauce thickens. Serve over noodles.

Chicken Vindaloo

Makes 4 servings

1 onion, coarsely chopped

⅓ cup white vinegar

2 tablespoons tomato paste

1 tablespoon minced fresh ginger

3 cloves garlic

1½ teaspoons paprika

1 teaspoon salt

1 teaspoon ground coriander

1 teaspoon ground turmeric

½ teaspoon dry mustard

½ teaspoon ground red pepper

½ teaspoon ground cumin

1½ pounds boneless skinless chicken thighs

¼ cup water

Hot cooked rice (optional)

Chopped fresh cilantro (optional)

1 Combine onion, vinegar, tomato paste, ginger, garlic, paprika, salt, coriander, turmeric, mustard, red pepper and cumin in food processor or blender; process until smooth.

2 Place chicken in large resealable food storage bag. Pour spice mixture over chicken; seal bag and massage mixture into chicken, making sure all pieces are completely coated. Marinate in refrigerator at least 1 hour or overnight.

3 Pour chicken and marinade into Instant Pot; stir in water. Secure lid and move pressure release valve to Sealing position. Press Pressure Cook or Manual; cook at high pressure 7 minutes.

4 When cooking is complete, use natural release for 5 minutes, then release remaining pressure. Remove chicken to plate; tent with foil to keep warm.

5 Press Sauté; cook about 5 minutes or until sauce reduces and thickens slightly, stirring frequently. Pour sauce over chicken; serve with rice, if desired. Garnish with cilantro.

Chicken Tinga

Makes 6 servings

1 tablespoon vegetable oil

1 medium white onion, quartered

3 medium tomatillos, husks removed and cut in half

3 cloves garlic

1 teaspoon dried oregano

½ teaspoon ground cumin

1 can (about 14 ounces) diced fire-roasted tomatoes

2 canned chipotle peppers in adobo sauce

2 tablespoons cider vinegar

1¼ teaspoons salt

2 pounds boneless skinless chicken thighs

2 bay leaves

Corn tortillas, heated

Optional toppings: pickled red onion, chopped fresh cilantro, shredded cabbage, diced avocado, lime wedges

1 Press Sauté; heat oil in Instant Pot. Add onion, tomatillos and garlic, cut sides down; cook about 5 minutes without stirring or until vegetables are browned in spots. Stir vegetables; cook 3 minutes for additional browning. Add oregano and cumin; cook and stir 1 minute. Add tomatoes; cook and stir 2 minutes. Stir in chipotle peppers, vinegar and salt; mix well.

2 Use hand-held immersion blender to purée mixure in pot until smooth (you will need to tilt pot for blending). Or transfer mixture to blender or food processor; blend until smooth and return to pot.

3 Add chicken and bay leaves to pot, submerging chicken in sauce. Secure lid and move pressure release valve to Sealing position. Cook at high pressure 8 minutes.

4 When cooking is complete, use natural release for 5 minutes, then release remaining pressure. Remove chicken to medium bowl; set aside 10 minutes or until cool enough to handle. Meanwhile, press Sauté; cook 5 minutes or until sauce reduces slightly. Remove and discard bay leaves.

5 Shred chicken into bite-size pieces. Add about half of sauce from pot; toss to coat. (Reserve leftover sauce for another use.) Serve with tortillas and desired toppings.

Turkey Ropa Vieja

Makes 4 servings

1 tablespoon olive oil

1 onion, thinly sliced

1 green bell pepper, chopped

1 clove garlic, minced

¾ teaspoon ground cumin

½ teaspoon dried oregano

2 medium tomatoes, chopped

1 can (8 ounces) tomato sauce

⅓ cup sliced pimiento-stuffed green olives

½ teaspoon salt

¼ teaspoon black pepper

1 pound turkey tenderloins (2 large or 3 small) *or* 1½ pounds boneless turkey breast, cut into 3 to 4 pieces

1 tablespoon lemon juice

Hot cooked rice and beans (optional)

1 Press Sauté; heat oil in Instant Pot. Add onion and bell pepper; cook and stir 3 minutes or until softened. Add garlic, cumin and oregano; cook and stir 30 seconds. Stir in tomatoes, tomato sauce, olives, salt and black pepper; mix well. Add turkey to pot, pressing into tomato mixture.

2 Secure lid and move pressure release valve to Sealing position. Press Pressure Cook or Manual; cook at high pressure 20 minutes.

3 When cooking is complete, use natural release for 10 minutes, then release remaining pressure. Remove turkey to plate.

4 Press Sauté; cook 10 to 15 minutes or until sauce is reduced by one third.

5 Meanwhile, shred turkey into bite-size pieces when cool enough to handle. Add shredded turkey and lemon juice to sauce; mix well. Serve with rice and beans, if desired.

Artichoke Dijon Chicken Thighs

Makes 4 to 6 servings

1 jar (12 ounces) quartered marinated artichoke hearts, undrained

1/3 cup Dijon mustard

2 tablespoons minced garlic

1/2 teaspoon dried tarragon

1/4 teaspoon salt

2 1/2 pounds bone-in chicken thighs, skin removed

1 1/2 cups thickly sliced mushrooms

1 cup chopped onion

2 tablespoons water

1 tablespoon all-purpose flour

1/4 cup chopped fresh parsley

Hot cooked pasta (optional)

1 Drain artichokes, reserving 1/2 cup marinade. (Discard remaining marinade.) Combine reserved marinade, mustard, garlic, tarragon and salt in Instant Pot; mix well. Add chicken, mushrooms and onion; stir to coat.

2 Secure lid and move pressure release valve to Sealing position. Press Pressure Cook or Manual; cook at high pressure 11 minutes. When cooking is complete, use natural release for 10 minutes, then release remaining pressure.

3 Remove chicken to plate; tent with foil. Press Sauté; add artichokes to pot. Cook about 5 minutes or until sauce is reduced by half and artichokes are heated through, stirring occasionally.

4 Stir water into flour in small bowl until smooth. Add to sauce; cook and stir 1 minute or until sauce thickens. Stir in parsley. Serve chicken and sauce over pasta, if desired.

Spanish Chicken and Rice

Makes 6 servings

- 2 tablespoons olive oil
- 1 package (about 12 ounces) kielbasa sausage, cut into ½-inch slices
- 2 pounds boneless skinless chicken thighs
- 1 onion, chopped
- 4 cloves garlic, minced
- 2 cups uncooked converted long grain rice
- 1 red bell pepper, diced
- ½ cup diced carrots
- ¾ teaspoon salt
- ¼ teaspoon black pepper
- ¼ teaspoon saffron threads (optional)
- 3 cups chicken broth
- ½ cup thawed frozen peas

1 Press Sauté; heat oil in Instant Pot. Add sausage; cook about 6 minutes or until browned. Remove to plate. Add chicken to pot in batches; cook about 8 minutes or until browned on both sides. Remove to plate.

2 Add onion to pot; cook and stir 3 minutes or until softened. Add garlic; cook and stir 30 seconds. Add rice, bell pepper, carrots, salt, black pepper and saffron, if desired; cook and stir 3 minutes. Stir in broth, scraping up browned bits from bottom of pot. Return chicken and sausage to pot, pressing chicken into liquid.

3 Secure lid and move pressure release valve to Sealing position. Press Pressure Cook or Manual; cook at high pressure 7 minutes.

4 When cooking is complete, use quick release. Remove chicken to clean plate; tent with foil.

5 Stir in peas; cover and let stand 2 minutes or until peas are heated through. Serve chicken over rice mixture.

Indian-Style Apricot Chicken

Makes 4 to 6 servings

2½ pounds bone-in chicken thighs, skin removed

½ teaspoon salt

¼ teaspoon black pepper

1 tablespoon vegetable oil

1 large onion, chopped

½ cup chicken broth, divided

1 tablespoon grated fresh ginger

2 cloves garlic, minced

½ teaspoon ground cinnamon

⅛ teaspoon ground allspice

1 can (about 14 ounces) diced tomatoes

1 package (8 ounces) dried apricots

Pinch saffron threads (optional)

Hot cooked basmati rice (optional)

Chopped fresh Italian parsley (optional)

1 Season both sides of chicken with ½ teaspoon salt and ¼ teaspoon pepper. Press Sauté; heat oil in Instant Pot. Add chicken in batches; cook about 8 minutes or until browned on both sides. Remove to plate.

2 Add onion and 2 tablespoons broth to pot; cook and stir 5 minutes or until onion is translucent, scraping up browned bits from bottom of pot. Add ginger, garlic, cinnamon and allspice; cook and stir 30 seconds or until fragrant. Stir in tomatoes, apricots, remaining broth and saffron, if desired; mix well. Return chicken to pot, pressing into liquid.

3 Secure lid and move pressure release valve to Sealing position. Press Pressure Cook or Manual; cook at high pressure 11 minutes.

4 When cooking is complete, use quick release. Season with additional salt and pepper. Serve with rice, if desired. Garnish with parsley.

Chicken Congee

Makes 6 servings

4 cups water

4 cups chicken broth

2 chicken leg quarters *or* 4 chicken drumsticks, skin removed (1 to 1½ pounds)

1 cup uncooked white jasmine rice, rinsed well and drained

1 (1-inch) piece fresh ginger, cut into ¼-inch slices

1 teaspoon salt

½ teaspoon white pepper

Optional toppings: soy sauce, sesame oil, sliced green onions, shredded carrot, salted roasted peanuts and/or pickled vegetables

1 Combine water, broth, chicken, rice, ginger, salt and pepper in Instant Pot; mix well.

2 Secure lid and move pressure release valve to Sealing position. Press Pressure Cook or Manual; cook at high pressure 20 minutes.

3 When cooking is complete, use natural release for 15 minutes, then release remaining pressure. Remove and discard ginger. Remove chicken to plate; set aside until cool enough to handle.

4 Meanwhile, press Sauté; cook and stir congee 2 to 3 minutes or until desired consistency is reached. Remove chicken meat from bones; discard bones. Shred chicken; stir into congee. Serve with desired toppings.

Pesto Turkey Meatballs

Makes 4 servings

- 1 pound ground turkey
- ⅓ cup prepared pesto
- ⅓ cup grated Parmesan cheese, plus additional for garnish
- ¼ cup panko bread crumbs
- 1 egg
- 2 green onions, finely chopped
- ½ teaspoon salt, divided
- 2 tablespoons olive oil
- 2 cloves garlic, minced
- ⅛ teaspoon red pepper flakes
- 1 can (28 ounces) whole tomatoes, undrained, coarsely chopped or crushed with hands
- 1 tablespoon tomato paste
- Hot cooked pasta (optional)
- Chopped fresh basil (optional)

1. Combine turkey, pesto, ⅓ cup cheese, panko, egg, green onions and ¼ teaspoon salt in medium bowl; mix well. Shape mixture into 24 (1¼-inch) meatballs. Refrigerate meatballs while preparing sauce.

2. Press Sauté; heat oil in Instant Pot. Add garlic and red pepper flakes; cook and stir 1 minute. Add tomatoes with liquid, tomato paste and remaining ¼ teaspoon salt; cook 3 minutes or until sauce begins to simmer, stirring occasionally.

3. Remove about 1 cup sauce from pot. Arrange meatballs in single layer in pot; pour reserved sauce over meatballs.

4. Secure lid and move pressure release valve to Sealing position. Press Pressure Cook or Manual; cook at high pressure 10 minutes.

5. When cooking is complete, use natural release for 10 minutes, then release remaining pressure. If sauce is too thin, press Sauté and cook 5 minutes or until sauce thickens, stirring frequently. Serve meatballs over pasta, if desired. Garnish with additional cheese and basil.

Black and White Chili

Makes 4 servings

- 1 tablespoon vegetable oil
- 1 pound chicken tenders, cut into 3/4-inch pieces
- 1 cup coarsely chopped onion
- 1 can (about 14 ounces) fire-roasted diced tomatoes
- 1 can (about 15 ounces) Great Northern beans, rinsed and drained
- 1 can (about 15 ounces) black beans, rinsed and drained
- 2 tablespoons chili seasoning mix
- 1/2 teaspoon salt
  Hot pepper sauce (optional)

1 Press Sauté; heat oil in Instant Pot. Add chicken and onion; cook and stir 5 minutes or until chicken begins to brown. Stir in tomatoes; cook 1 minute, scraping up browned bits from bottom of pot. Stir in beans, chili seasoning mix and salt; mix well.

2 Secure lid and move pressure release valve to Sealing position. Press Pressure Cook or Manual; cook at high pressure 5 minutes.

3 When cooking is complete, use natural release for 10 minutes, then release remaining pressure. Serve with hot pepper sauce, if desired.

BEEF & PORK

Italian Beef Ragu
Makes 6 servings

2 pounds beef chuck roast, cut into 2-inch pieces

½ teaspoon salt

½ teaspoon black pepper

1 tablespoon olive oil

1 onion, chopped

½ cup plus 2 tablespoons beef broth, divided

1 jar (24 ounces) garlic and herb pasta sauce

¼ cup plus 1 tablespoon red wine vinegar, divided

   Hot cooked pappardelle pasta

1 Season beef with ½ teaspoon salt and ½ teaspoon pepper. Press Sauté; heat oil in Instant Pot. Add beef in two batches; cook about 5 minutes or until browned. Remove to plate. Add onion and 2 tablespoons broth; cook and stir 3 minutes or until softened, scraping up browned bits from bottom of pot. Reserve ¾ cup pasta sauce; set aside. Add remaining pasta sauce, ½ cup broth and ¼ cup vinegar to pot; mix well. Return beef and accumulated juices to pot; stir to coat.

2 Secure lid and move pressure release valve to Sealing position. Press Pressure Cook or Manual; cook at high pressure 45 minutes.

3 When cooking is complete, use natural release for 15 minutes, then release remaining pressure. Remove beef to large bowl; let stand 5 minutes or until cool enough to handle.

4 Meanwhile, press Sauté; adjust heat to low. Add reserved ¾ cup pasta sauce and remaining 1 tablespoon vinegar to pot; cook 5 minutes, stirring occasionally.

5 Shred beef; stir into sauce. Taste and season with additional salt and pepper, if desired. Serve over pasta.

Perfect BBQ Ribs

Makes 4 servings

1 rack pork baby back ribs (about 3 pounds)

⅓ cup barbecue seasoning or grilling rub

2 cups apple juice

¼ cup cider vinegar

1 tablespoon liquid smoke

1 cup barbecue sauce, plus additional for serving

1 Remove membrane covering bones on underside of ribs. Rub barbecue seasoning generously over both sides of ribs, pressing to adhere.

2 Combine apple juice, vinegar and liquid smoke in Instant Pot; mix well. Stand ribs vertically in liquid, coiling ribs into a ring to fit in pot.

3 Secure lid and move pressure release valve to Sealing position. Cook at high pressure 20 minutes. Preheat broiler. Line baking sheet with foil.

4 When cooking is complete, use natural release for 5 minutes, then release remaining pressure. Remove ribs to prepared baking sheet, meaty side up. Brush both sides of ribs with 1 cup barbecue sauce.

5 Broil about 5 minutes or until sauce begins to bubble and char. Cut into individual ribs; serve with additional sauce.

Quick French Dip
Makes 6 servings

3 pounds boneless beef chuck roast

½ teaspoon salt

½ teaspoon black pepper

1 tablespoon olive oil

2 onions, cut in half and cut into ¼-inch slices

⅔ cup reduced-sodium beef broth

3 tablespoons Worcestershire sauce

6 hoagie rolls, split

12 slices provolone cheese

1 Season beef with salt and pepper. Press Sauté; heat oil in Instant Pot. Add beef; cook about 6 minutes per side or until well browned. Remove to cutting board.

2 Add onions to pot; cook 6 to 8 minutes or until golden brown, stirring occasionally. Remove half of onions to small bowl; set aside. Add broth and Worcestershire sauce to pot; mix well. Cut beef into 3-inch pieces; add to pot and turn to coat.

3 Secure lid and move pressure release valve to Sealing position. Press Pressure Cook or Manual; cook at high pressure 45 minutes.

4 When cooking is complete, use natural release for 15 minutes, then release remaining pressure. Remove beef to large bowl; let stand until cool enough to handle. Shred into bite-size pieces. Add ⅔ cup cooking liquid; toss to coat. Strain remaining cooking liquid for serving, if desired. Preheat broiler. Line baking sheet with foil.

5 Place rolls cut sides up on prepared baking sheet; broil until lightly browned. Top bottom halves of rolls with cheese, beef and reserved onions. Serve with warm au jus for dipping.

Chorizo Burritos

Makes 4 servings

15 ounces uncooked Mexican chorizo sausages, cut into bite-size pieces

2 green or red bell peppers, cut into 1-inch pieces

1 can (about 15 ounces) red beans, rinsed and drained

1 can (about 14 ounces) diced tomatoes

1 can (11 ounces) corn, drained

½ teaspoon ground cumin

½ teaspoon ground cinnamon

8 (8-inch) flour tortillas, warmed

2 cups hot cooked rice

½ cup (2 ounces) shredded Monterey Jack cheese

1 Combine chorizo, bell peppers, beans, tomatoes, corn, cumin and cinnamon in Instant Pot; mix well.

2 Secure lid and move pressure release valve to Sealing position. Cook at high pressure 10 minutes.

3 When cooking is complete, use natural release for 10 minutes, then release remaining pressure.

4 Press Sauté; cook about 5 minutes or until chorizo mixture thickens, stirring occasionally.

5 Spoon chorizo mixture down centers of tortillas; top with rice and shredded cheese. Roll up tortillas; serve immediately.

Instant Spaghetti and Meatballs

Makes 6 servings

1 pound frozen meatballs

8 ounces uncooked spaghetti, broken in half

1 tablespoon olive oil

3/4 teaspoon salt

2 cups water

1 jar (24 ounces) chunky marinara sauce

Grated Parmesan cheese and fresh basil leaves (optional)

1 Place meatballs in single layer in Instant Pot. Arrange pasta in criss-crossing layers over meatballs; drizzle with oil.

2 Stir salt into water in measuring cup. Pour marinara sauce and water over pasta, making sure to cover pasta completely.

3 Secure lid and move pressure release valve to Sealing position. Cook at high pressure 9 minutes.

4 When cooking is complete, use quick release. Gently stir with tongs to separate pasta and blend with sauce. Garnish with cheese and basil.

Pork Roast with Tart Cherries

Makes 4 servings

- 3 teaspoons grated horseradish, divided
- 2 teaspoons ground coriander
- ¾ teaspoon salt
- ½ teaspoon black pepper
- 1 tablespoon olive oil
- 1 boneless pork loin roast (about 2 pounds), trimmed
- 1 can (about 14 ounces) pitted tart cherries, undrained
- ¼ cup dry sherry, Madeira or white wine
- 4 teaspoons grated orange peel
- 1 tablespoon packed brown sugar
- 1 tablespoon Dijon mustard
- ⅛ teaspoon ground cloves
  Orange slices (optional)
  Fresh Italian parsley sprigs (optional)

1. Combine 2 teaspoons horseradish, coriander, salt and pepper in small bowl; mix well. Press Sauté; heat oil in Instant Pot. Add pork; cook about 10 minutes or until browned on all sides. Remove to plate; rub horseradish mixture evenly over all sides of pork.

2. Drain cherries, reserving ¼ cup liquid. Add cherries, reserved cherry liquid and sherry to pot; cook about 4 minutes or until half of liquid is evaporated, scraping up browned bits from bottom of pot. Place rack in pot; place pork on rack.

3. Secure lid and move pressure release valve to Sealing position. Press Pressure Cook or Manual; cook at high pressure 25 minutes.

4. When cooking is complete, use natural release for 10 minutes, then release remaining pressure. Remove pork to plate; tent with foil.

5. Strain cooking liquid into medium bowl, reserving cherries. Return liquid to pot. Press Sauté; stir in orange peel, brown sugar, mustard, remaining 1 teaspoon horseradish and cloves. Cook 10 minutes or until sauce thickens slightly, stirring occasionally. Stir in reserved cherries. Serve sauce with pork; garnish with orange slices and parsley.

Tip

For a spicier pork roast, double the amount of the horseradish, coriander, and pepper used for the rub.

Barbecue Beef Sandwiches

Makes 4 servings

2½ pounds boneless beef chuck roast, cut in half

2 tablespoons Southwest seasoning

1 tablespoon vegetable oil

½ cup beef broth

1½ cups barbecue sauce, divided

4 sandwich or pretzel buns, split

1⅓ cups prepared coleslaw* (preferably vinegar based)

*Prepared coleslaw can be found in the deli department at most supermarkets. Vinegar-based coleslaws provide a perfect complement to the rich beef; they can often be found at the salad bar or prepared foods section of large supermarkets.

1 Sprinkle both sides of beef with Southwest seasoning. Press Sauté; heat oil in Instant Pot. Add beef; cook about 6 minutes per side or until browned. Remove to plate.

2 Add broth to pot; cook 2 minutes, scraping up browned bits from bottom of pot. Stir in ½ cup barbecue sauce. Return beef to pot; turn to coat.

3 Secure lid and move pressure release valve to Sealing position. Press Pressure Cook or Manual; cook at high pressure 60 minutes.

4 When cooking is complete, use natural release for 15 minutes, then release remaining pressure. Remove beef to large bowl; let stand until cool enough to handle. Shred beef into bite-size pieces. Stir in remaining 1 cup barbecue sauce.

5 Fill buns with beef mixture; top with coleslaw.

Old-Fashioned Meat Loaf

Makes 6 servings

1 tablespoon olive oil

1 small onion, finely chopped

½ red bell pepper, finely chopped

3 cloves garlic, minced

1 teaspoon dried oregano

1½ cups water

2 pounds ground meat loaf mix *or* 1 pound each ground beef and ground pork

1 egg

3 tablespoons tomato paste

1 teaspoon salt

½ teaspoon black pepper

1 Press Sauté; heat oil in Instant Pot. Add onion, bell pepper, garlic and oregano; cook and stir 3 minutes or until vegetables are softened. Remove to large bowl; let cool 5 minutes. Wipe out pot with paper towels; add water and rack to pot.

2 Add meat loaf mix, egg, tomato paste, salt and black pepper to vegetable mixture; mix well. Tear off 18×12-inch piece of foil; fold in half crosswise to create 12×9-inch rectangle. Shape meat mixture into 7×5-inch oval on foil; bring up sides of foil to create pan, leaving top of meat loaf uncovered. Place foil with meat loaf on rack in pot.

3 Secure lid and move pressure release valve to Sealing position. Press Pressure Cook or Manual; cook at high pressure 37 minutes.

4 When cooking is complete, use quick release. Remove meat loaf to cutting board; tent with foil. Let stand 10 minutes before slicing.

Irish Beef Stew

Makes 6 servings

2½ tablespoons vegetable oil, divided

2 pounds boneless beef chuck roast, cut into 1-inch pieces

1½ teaspoons salt, divided

¾ teaspoon black pepper, divided

1 package (8 to 10 ounces) cremini mushrooms, quartered

1 medium onion, quartered

1 cup Guinness stout

1 tablespoon Dijon mustard

1 tablespoon tomato paste

1 tablespoon Worcestershire sauce

2 cloves garlic, minced

2 bay leaves

1 teaspoon dried thyme

1 teaspoon dried rosemary

1 pound small yellow potatoes (about 1¼ inches), halved

3 medium carrots, cut into ¾-inch pieces

3 medium parsnips, cut into ¾-inch pieces

2 teaspoons water

2 teaspoons cornstarch

1 cup frozen pearl onions

Chopped fresh parsley (optional)

1 Press Sauté; heat 2 tablespoons oil in Instant Pot. Season beef with 1 teaspoon salt and ½ teaspoon pepper. Cook beef in two batches about 5 minutes or until browned. Remove to plate.

2 Add remaining ½ tablespoon oil, mushrooms and onion quarters to pot; cook about 6 minutes or until mushrooms release their liquid and begin to brown, stirring frequently. Add Guinness, mustard, tomato paste, Worcestershire sauce, garlic, bay leaves, thyme, rosemary, remaining ½ teaspoon salt and ¼ teaspoon pepper; cook and stir 3 minutes, scraping up browned bits from bottom of pot. Return beef and any accumulated juices to pot; mix well.

3 Secure lid and move pressure release valve to Sealing position. Press Pressure Cook or Manual; cook at high pressure 30 minutes.

4 When cooking is complete, use quick release. Remove and discard bay leaves and large onion pieces. Add potatoes, carrots and parsnips to pot; mix well. Secure lid and move pressure release valve to Sealing position. Cook at high pressure 3 minutes. Meanwhile, stir water into cornstarch in small bowl until smooth.

5 When cooking is complete, use quick release. Press Sauté; stir pearl onions into stew. Add cornstarch mixture; cook 2 to 3 minutes or until stew thickens, stirring frequently. Garnish with parsley.

Tacos al Pastor

Makes about 6 servings

1 medium pineapple

1 small red onion, coarsely chopped

   Juice of 1 orange

   Juice of 1 lime

2 canned chipotle peppers in adobo sauce

1 tablespoon white vinegar

1 tablespoon chili powder

2 teaspoons salt

2 cloves garlic

1 teaspoon ground cumin

½ teaspoon black pepper

2½ pounds boneless pork shoulder, cut into 2-inch pieces

   Flour or corn tortillas, heated

   Optional toppings: chopped or pickled red onion, chopped fresh cilantro, diced avocado, lime wedges

1 Peel and core pineapple; set aside half for topping. Coarsely chop remaining half; place in food processor with onion, orange juice, lime juice, chipotle peppers, vinegar, chili powder, salt, garlic, cumin and black pepper. Process until smooth.

2 Place pork in large resealable food storage bag; pour marinade over pork. Seal bag and turn to coat. Marinate in refrigerator at least 4 hours or overnight.

3 Pour pork and marinade into Instant Pot. Secure lid and move pressure release valve to Sealing position. Cook at high pressure 40 minutes.

4 Meanwhile, cut remaining half of pineapple into ½-inch pieces. Preheat broiler. Line baking sheet with foil. Spread pineapple on one third of baking sheet.

5 When cooking is complete, use natural release for 10 minutes, then release remaining pressure. Remove pork to prepared baking sheet; break into smaller chunks and spread out next to pineapple. Broil 5 to 8 minutes or until pork and pineapple begin to brown and char in spots.

6 Meanwhile, press Sauté; cook liquid in pot 5 to 10 minutes or until sauce reduces and thickens slightly. Drizzle sauce over pork; serve pork and pineapple in tortillas with desired toppings.

Brisket Tacos

Makes about 6 servings

2 teaspoons salt

2 teaspoons chili powder

2 teaspoons smoked paprika

1 teaspoon ground cumin

½ teaspoon black pepper

1 small beef brisket (2½ to 3 pounds), trimmed

3 tablespoons vegetable oil, divided

2 medium onions, cut in half and cut into ¼-inch slices, divided

¾ cup beef broth, divided

3 cloves garlic, minced

2 medium poblano peppers, cut into ¼-inch slices

Corn tortillas, heated

Optional toppings: sliced red cabbage or slaw, fresh cilantro leaves, sliced avocado, pickled red onions, shredded Monterey Jack cheese

1 Combine salt, chili powder, smoked paprika, cumin and black pepper in small bowl; mix well. Pat brisket dry; cut in half crosswise. Rub spice mixture over all sides to coat completely. Let stand at room temperature 30 minutes or cover and refrigerate overnight.

2 Press Sauté; heat 1 tablespoon oil in Instant Pot. Add one brisket half, fat side down; cook 3 to 4 minutes per side or until browned. Remove to plate. Repeat with 1 tablespoon oil and remaining brisket half. Add 1 onion and 2 tablespoons broth to pot; cook 3 minutes or until softened, scraping up browned bits from bottom of pot. Add garlic; cook and stir 1 minute. Stir in remaining broth; mix well. Return brisket to pot. Secure lid and move pressure release valve to Sealing position. Press Pressure Cook or Manual; cook at high pressure 1 hour 15 minutes.

3 When cooking is complete, use natural release. Remove brisket to large plate; let stand 10 minutes. Meanwhile, preheat broiler. Line baking sheet with foil. Combine remaining onion and poblano peppers on prepared baking sheet. Drizzle with remaining 1 tablespoon oil and 2 tablespoons cooking liquid from pot; toss to coat. Spread vegetables on baking sheet. Broil 6 to 8 minutes or until vegetables begin to brown, stirring occasionally. Remove to bowl.

4 Shred brisket into bite-size pieces; transfer to same baking sheet. Drizzle with ⅓ cup cooking liquid from pot; toss to coat. Spread out meat on baking sheet. Broil about 5 minutes or until edges begin to char. Toss with additional cooking liquid, if desired.

5 Serve brisket and vegetables in tortillas with desired toppings.

Italian Beef Sandwiches

Makes 4 servings

1 jar (16 ounces) sliced pepperoncini

1 jar (16 ounces) giardiniera

2 to 2½ pounds boneless beef chuck roast

½ cup beef broth

1 tablespoon Italian seasoning

4 French or sub rolls, split

1 Drain pepperoncini, reserving ½ cup liquid. Set aside ½ cup pepperoncini for sandwiches. Drain giardiniera, reserving ½ cup vegetables for sandwiches.

2 Combine beef, remaining pepperoncini and reserved ½ cup pepperoncini liquid, remaining giardiniera vegetables, broth and Italian seasoning in Instant Pot.

3 Secure lid and move pressure release valve to Sealing position. Cook at high pressure 60 minutes.

4 When cooking is complete, use natural release for 15 minutes, then release remaining pressure. Remove beef to large bowl; let stand until cool enough to handle. Shred into bite-size pieces. Add ½ cup cooking liquid; toss to coat.

5 Fill rolls with beef, reserved pepperoncini and reserved giardiniera vegetables. Serve with warm cooking liquid for dipping.

Bacon and Stout Short Ribs

Makes 4 to 6 servings

6 slices thick-cut bacon, chopped

4 pounds bone-in beef short ribs, trimmed and cut into 3-inch pieces

1 teaspoon salt, divided

½ teaspoon black pepper

1 large onion, cut in half and thinly sliced

1 tablespoon tomato paste

1 bottle or can (12 ounces) stout, dark beer or ale

2 tablespoons spicy brown mustard

1 bay leaf

3 tablespoons water

2 tablespoons all-purpose flour

2 tablespoons finely chopped fresh parsley

Hot mashed potatoes or cooked egg noodles (optional)

1 Press Sauté; cook bacon in Instant Pot until crisp. Remove to paper towel-lined plate. Drain off all but 1 tablespoon drippings.

2 Season short ribs with ½ teaspoon salt and pepper. Add short ribs to pot in batches; cook about 8 minutes or until browned on all sides. Remove to plate. Drain off all but 1 tablespoon fat.

3 Add onion to pot; cook and stir 5 minutes or until golden brown. Add tomato paste; cook and stir 1 minute. Add stout, mustard, bay leaf and remaining ½ teaspoon salt; cook and stir 1 minute, scraping up browned bits from bottom of pot. Return bacon and short ribs to pot.

4 Secure lid and move pressure release valve to Sealing position. Press Pressure Cook or Manual; cook at high pressure 45 minutes.

5 When cooking is complete, use natural release for 10 minutes, then release remaining pressure. Remove short ribs to clean plate; tent with foil. Remove and discard bay leaf.

6 Skim excess fat from surface of sauce. Stir water into flour in small bowl until smooth. Press Sauté; add flour mixture to cooking liquid in pot, stirring constantly. Cook and stir about 5 minutes or until sauce thickens. Stir in parsley. Serve sauce with short ribs and mashed potatoes, if desired.

Chili Verde
Makes 4 servings

- 1 tablespoon vegetable oil
- 1 pound boneless pork loin, cut into 1-inch pieces
- 1 onion, cut in half and thinly sliced
- 1 pound tomatillos, husks removed, rinsed and coarsely chopped
- 6 cloves garlic, minced
- 1 teaspoon ground cumin
- 1 can (about 15 ounces) Great Northern beans, rinsed and drained
- 1 can (4 ounces) diced green chiles
- 1 teaspoon salt
- ¼ teaspoon black pepper
- ¼ cup chopped fresh cilantro

1 Press Sauté; heat oil in Instant Pot. Add pork; cook about 6 minutes or until browned, stirring occasionally. Remove to plate.

2 Add onion to pot; cook and stir 3 minutes or until softened. Add tomatillos, garlic and cumin; cook and stir 3 minutes, scraping up browned bits from bottom of pot. Stir in beans, chiles, salt, pepper and pork; mix well.

3 Secure lid and move pressure release valve to Sealing position. Press Pressure Cook or Manual; cook at high pressure 8 minutes.

4 When cooking is complete, use natural release for 10 minutes, then release remaining pressure. Stir in cilantro.

Creole-Spiced Pot Roast

Makes 6 servings

2 tablespoons Creole or Cajun seasoning

1 boneless beef chuck roast (3 pounds), cut in half

1 tablespoon vegetable oil

1 medium onion, chopped

1 can (about 14 ounces) diced tomatoes, drained

1 can (about 14 ounces) diced tomatoes with green chiles, drained

2 tablespoons hot pepper sauce

1 teaspoon sugar

½ teaspoon black pepper

1 cup chopped rutabaga

1 cup chopped mushrooms

1 cup chopped turnip

1 cup chopped parsnip

1 cup chopped green bell pepper

1 cup green beans

1 cup sliced carrots

1 cup corn

1 Rub Creole seasoning into all sides of beef. Press Sauté; heat oil in Instant Pot. Add beef; cook about 10 minutes or until browned on all sides. Add onion to pot during last few minutes of cooking, stirring until softened. Add tomatoes, hot pepper sauce, sugar and black pepper; mix well.

2 Secure lid and move pressure release valve to Sealing position. Press Pressure Cook or Manual; cook at high pressure 65 minutes.

3 When cooking is complete, use quick release. Add rutabaga, mushrooms, turnip, parsnip, bell pepper, beans, carrots and corn to pot, pressing vegetables down into liquid.

4 Secure lid and move pressure release valve to sealing or locked position. Cook at high pressure 10 minutes.

5 When cooking is complete, use quick release.

Taco Salad
Makes 4 servings

Chili

1	pound ground beef
1	medium onion, chopped
1	stalk celery, chopped
2	medium tomatoes, chopped
1	jalapeño pepper, finely chopped
1½	teaspoons chili powder
1	teaspoon salt
1	teaspoon ground cumin
½	teaspoon black pepper
1	can (15 ounces) tomato sauce
1	can (about 15 ounces) kidney beans, rinsed and drained
1	can (about 15 ounces) pinto beans, rinsed and drained
½	cup water

Salad

8	cups chopped romaine lettuce (large pieces)
2	cups diced fresh tomatoes
2	cups small tortilla chips
	Optional toppings: salsa, sour cream, shredded Cheddar cheese

1 Press Sauté; add beef to Instant Pot. Cook about 8 minutes or until browned, stirring frequently. Drain off fat and excess liquid. Add onion and celery to pot; cook and stir 3 minutes.

2 Add chopped tomatoes, jalapeño, chili powder, salt, cumin and black pepper; cook and stir 1 minute. Stir in tomato sauce, beans and water; mix well.

3 Secure lid and move pressure release valve to Sealing position. Press Pressure Cook or Manual; cook at high pressure 20 minutes.

4 When cooking is complete, use natural release for 10 minutes, then release remaining pressure.

5 For each salad, combine 2 cups lettuce and ½ cup diced tomatoes in individual bowl. Top with tortilla chips, chili, salsa, sour cream and cheese, if desired. (Recipe makes more chili than needed for salads; reserve remaining chili for another use.)

Chili Spiced Pork Loin

Makes 4 servings

1 boneless pork loin roast
(2 to 2½ pounds), trimmed
1¼ cups orange juice, divided
1 cup chopped onion
2 cloves garlic, minced
1 tablespoon cider vinegar
1½ teaspoons chili powder
1 teaspoon salt
¼ teaspoon dried thyme
¼ teaspoon ground cumin
¼ teaspoon ground cinnamon
⅛ teaspoon ground allspice
⅛ teaspoon ground cloves
2 tablespoons olive oil
Fruit Chutney (recipe
follows, optional)

1 Place pork in large resealable food storage bag or glass dish. Combine ½ cup orange juice, onion, garlic, vinegar, chili powder, salt, thyme, cumin, cinnamon, allspice and cloves in small bowl; mix well. Pour marinade over pork; seal bag and turn to coat. Refrigerate 2 to 4 hours or overnight.

2 Remove pork from marinade; reserve marinade. Press Sauté; heat oil in Instant Pot. Add pork; cook about 6 minutes or until browned on all sides. Stir in remaining ¾ cup orange juice and reserved marinade, scraping up browned bits from bottom of pot.

3 Secure lid and move pressure release valve to Sealing position. Press Pressure Cook or Manual; cook at high pressure 20 minutes.

4 When cooking is complete, use natural release for 10 minutes, then release remaining pressure. Remove pork to cutting board; tent with foil. Let stand 10 minutes before slicing.

5 Meanwhile, prepare Fruit Chutney, if desired. Or press Sauté; cook until liquid in pot is reduced by one third. Serve with pork.

Fruit Chutney

Add ¼ cup apricot preserves or orange marmalade to cooking liquid after removing pork from pot. Press Sauté; cook 10 minutes, stirring occasionally. Add 1 diced mango, ½ cup diced fresh pineapple, 2 minced green onions and 1 tablespoon minced jalapeño pepper; cook and stir 5 minutes. Serve with pork.

Simple Sloppy Joes

Makes 6 servings

1½ pounds ground beef
1 red bell pepper, chopped
½ cup chopped onion
1 clove garlic, minced
¼ cup ketchup
¼ cup barbecue sauce
2 tablespoons cider vinegar
1 tablespoon Worcestershire sauce
1 tablespoon packed brown sugar
1 teaspoon chili powder
1 can (about 8 ounces) baked beans
6 sandwich rolls, split
¾ cup (3 ounces) shredded Cheddar cheese (optional)

1 Press Sauté; add beef to Instant Pot. Cook about 8 minutes or until browned, stirring frequently. Drain off fat and excess liquid. Add bell pepper, onion and garlic to pot; cook and stir 3 minutes. Add ketchup, barbecue sauce, vinegar, Worcestershire sauce, brown sugar and chili powder; mix well.

2 Secure lid and move pressure release valve to Sealing position. Press Pressure Cook or Manual; cook at high pressure 10 minutes.

3 When cooking is complete, use quick release. Press Sauté; add beans to pot. Cook 5 minutes or until beef mixture thickens, stirring frequently.

4 Serve beef mixture on rolls; sprinkle with cheese, if desired.

Mole Chili

Makes 4 servings

2 tablespoons olive oil, divided

1½ pounds boneless beef chuck, cut into 1-inch pieces

2 medium onions, chopped

5 cloves garlic, minced

1 cup beef broth, divided

1 can (about 14 ounces) fire-roasted diced tomatoes

2 corn tortillas, each cut into 4 wedges

2 tablespoons chili powder

1 tablespoon ancho chili powder

1 teaspoon dried oregano

1 teaspoon ground cumin

¾ teaspoon salt

¾ teaspoon ground cinnamon

½ teaspoon black pepper

1 can (about 15 ounces) red kidney beans, rinsed and drained

1½ ounces semisweet chocolate, chopped

1 Press Sauté; heat 1 tablespoon oil in Instant Pot. Add beef in two batches; cook about 5 minutes or until browned. Remove to plate. Add remaining 1 tablespoon oil, onions and garlic to pot; cook and stir about 3 minutes or until onions are softened. Stir in ½ cup broth, scraping up browned bits from bottom of pot. Stir in remaining ½ cup broth, beef, tomatoes, tortillas, chili powders, oregano, cumin, salt, cinnamon and pepper; mix well.

2 Secure lid and move pressure release valve to Sealing position. Press Pressure Cook or Manual; cook at high pressure 30 minutes.

3 When cooking is complete, use natural release for 15 minutes, then release remaining pressure.

4 Press Sauté; add beans and chocolate to pot. Cook and stir 2 minutes or until chocolate is melted and beans are heated through.

BEANS & GRAINS

Pasta e Ceci

Makes 4 servings

1 cup dried chickpeas, soaked
    8 hours or overnight

3 tablespoons olive oil

1 onion, chopped

1 carrot, chopped

2 teaspoons salt

1 clove garlic, minced

1 teaspoon minced
    fresh rosemary

1 can (28 ounces) whole
    tomatoes, undrained,
    crushed with hands
    or coarsely chopped

2 cups vegetable broth
    or water

1 bay leaf

$1/8$ teaspoon red pepper flakes

1 cup uncooked orecchiette
    pasta

   Black pepper

   Chopped fresh parsley
   (optional)

1 Drain and rinse chickpeas. Press Sauté; heat oil in Instant Pot. Add onion and carrot; cook and stir 8 minutes or until vegetables are softened. Add salt, garlic and rosemary; cook and stir 1 minute. Add chickpeas, tomatoes with liquid, broth, bay leaf and red pepper flakes; mix well.

2 Secure lid and move pressure release valve to Sealing position. Press Pressure Cook or Manual; cook at high pressure 15 minutes. When cooking is complete, use natural release for 5 minutes, then release remaining pressure.

3 Stir in pasta. Secure lid and move pressure release valve to Sealing position. Press Pressure Cook or Manual; cook at high pressure 6 minutes.

4 When cooking is complete, use quick release. Remove and discard bay leaf. Season with black pepper; garnish with parsley.

Tip

To crush the tomatoes, take them out of the can one at a time and crush them between your fingers over the pot. Or coarsely chop them with a knife.

Shortcut Baked Beans

Makes 6 to 8 servings

5	slices thick-cut bacon, chopped
1	small onion, chopped
3½	cups water
1	pound dried pinto beans, rinsed and sorted
1	cup barbecue sauce
¼	cup ketchup
½	teaspoon salt

1 Press Sauté; cook bacon in Instant Pot until crisp. Drain off all but 1 tablespoon drippings.

2 Add onion to pot; cook and stir 3 minutes or until softened. Add water and beans; cook 1 minute, scraping up browned bits from bottom of pot. Stir in barbecue sauce and ketchup; mix well.

3 Secure lid and move pressure release valve to Sealing position. Press Pressure Cook or Manual; cook at high pressure 50 minutes.

4 When cooking is complete, use natural release for 15 minutes, then release remaining pressure. Stir beans; season with ½ teaspoon salt. If there is excess liquid in pot, press Sauté and cook 3 to 5 minutes or until liquid is reduced, stirring frequently.

Jalapeño Cheddar Cornbread
Makes 8 servings

1 cup yellow cornmeal

¾ cup all-purpose flour

⅓ cup sugar

2 teaspoons baking powder

1 teaspoon salt

1 cup buttermilk or whole milk

2 eggs

3 tablespoons butter, melted

1 cup (4 ounces) shredded Cheddar cheese

2 jalapeño peppers, seeded and minced (about ⅓ cup)

1½ cups water

1 Spray 7-inch springform pan with nonstick cooking spray. Combine cornmeal, flour, sugar, baking powder and salt in large bowl; mix well.

2 Beat buttermilk, eggs and butter in medium bowl until blended. Add to cornmeal mixture; stir just until blended. Stir in cheese and jalapeños until blended. Spread batter evenly in prepared pan; cover with foil.

3 Pour water into Instant Pot; place rack in pot. Place pan on rack. Secure lid and move pressure release valve to Sealing position. Press Pressure Cook or Manual; cook at high pressure 30 minutes.

4 When cooking is complete, use quick release. Remove pan from pot. Uncover; cool on wire rack 5 minutes before serving.

Spanish Rice
Makes 6 to 8 servings

1 tablespoon olive oil

1 small onion, chopped

2 cloves garlic, minced

2 cups uncooked brown rice, rinsed well and drained

1 can (about 14 ounces) diced tomatoes with green chiles

1 cup plus 2 tablespoons chicken broth or water

1 teaspoon salt

1 Press Sauté; heat oil in Instant Pot. Add onion and garlic; cook and stir 2 minutes. Add rice; cook and stir 2 minutes. Stir in tomatoes, broth and salt; mix well.

2 Secure lid and move pressure release valve to Sealing position. Press Pressure Cook or Manual; cook at high pressure 24 minutes.

3 When cooking is complete, use natural release for 10 minutes, then release remaining pressure. Fluff rice with fork.

Easy Cheesy Lasagna

Makes 4 to 6 servings

1 cup ricotta cheese

1¾ cups (7 ounces) shredded Italian blend cheese, divided

1 egg

2½ cups pasta sauce

8 no-boil lasagna noodles (about 5 ounces)

1½ cups water

1 Spray 7-inch springform pan with nonstick cooking spray. Beat ricotta, ½ cup shredded cheese and egg in small bowl until well blended.

2 Spread ½ cup pasta sauce on bottom of prepared pan. Top with 2 noodles, breaking to fit and cover sauce layer. Spread one third of ricotta mixture over sauce; top with ¼ cup shredded cheese. Repeat layers of sauce, noodles, ricotta mixture and shredded cheese twice, pressing down gently. Top with remaining 2 noodles, ½ cup pasta sauce and ½ cup shredded cheese. Cover pan with foil sprayed with nonstick cooking spray (or use nonstick foil).

3 Pour water into Instant Pot; place rack in pot. Place pan on rack. Secure lid and move pressure release valve to Sealing position. Press Pressure Cook or Manual; cook at high pressure 16 minutes. Preheat broiler.

4 When cooking is complete, use natural release for 5 minutes, then release remaining pressure. Remove pan from pot. Uncover; place lasagna on baking sheet. Broil about 3 minutes or until top is golden brown in spots.

Greek Giant Beans in Tomato Sauce

Makes about 8 cups

1 pound dried gigante beans* (about 2¼ cups)

1½ tablespoons salt, divided

2 bay leaves

¼ cup olive oil

2 small onions, chopped

1 stalk celery, finely chopped

1 medium carrot, finely chopped

3 cloves garlic, minced

1 teaspoon dried oregano, plus additional for serving

⅛ teaspoon red pepper flakes

1 can (28 ounces) whole tomatoes, undrained, coarsely chopped or crushed with hands

2 tablespoons tomato paste

½ teaspoon black pepper

Chopped fresh parsley

Crumbled feta cheese

If gigante beans are not available, use another variety of large white bean such as lima, butter or corona beans.

1 Rinse, drain and sort beans. Combine beans, 8 cups water and 1 tablespoon salt in medium bowl; soak 8 hours or overnight.

2 Drain beans; add to Instant Pot with 6 cups water and bay leaves. Secure lid and move pressure release valve to Sealing position. Press Pressure Cook or Manual; cook at high pressure 15 minutes. When cooking is complete, use natural release for 20 minutes, then release remaining pressure. Drain beans in colander, reserving 1 cup cooking liquid. Wipe out pot with paper towel.

3 Press Sauté; heat oil in pot. Add onions, celery and carrot; cook and stir 5 minutes or until vegetables are softened. Add garlic, 1 teaspoon oregano and red pepper flakes, cook and stir 30 seconds. Add tomatoes with liquid, tomato paste, remaining ½ tablespoon salt and black pepper; mix well. Stir in beans and ⅓ cup bean cooking liquid. Secure lid and move pressure release valve to Sealing position. Press Pressure Cook or Manual; cook at high pressure 5 minutes.

4 When cooking is complete, use natural release for 10 minutes, then release remaining pressure. If sauce is too thin, press Sauté; cook 5 minutes until sauce thickens and reduces slightly, stirring frequently. If sauce is too thick, stir in additional bean cooking liquid. Sprinkle with parsley, cheese and additional oregano.

Farro with Butternut Squash and Kale

Makes 6 to 8 servings

2 tablespoons olive oil

1 small red onion, chopped

2 cloves garlic, minced

½ teaspoon dried thyme

1½ cups uncooked farro, rinsed and drained

2 cups vegetable broth

1½ teaspoons salt

¼ teaspoon black pepper

1 small butternut squash (about 1½ pounds), peeled and cut into ¾-inch pieces (3 cups)

1 small bunch lacinato kale, stemmed and cut crosswise into 1-inch-wide strips (3 cups)

½ cup grated Parmesan cheese, divided

1 Press Sauté; heat oil in Instant Pot. Add onion; cook and stir 3 minutes or until softened. Add garlic and thyme; cook and stir 1 minute. Add farro; cook and stir 2 minutes. Stir in broth, salt and pepper; mix well.

2 Secure lid and move pressure release valve to Sealing position. Press Pressure Cook or Manual; cook at high pressure 7 minutes.

3 When cooking is complete, use quick release. Stir in squash and kale. Secure lid and move pressure release valve to Sealing position. Press Pressure Cook or Manual; cook at high pressure 3 minutes.

4 When cooking is complete, use natural release for 5 minutes, then release remaining pressure. Stir in half of cheese; serve with remaining cheese.

Cheese Grits with Chiles and Bacon

Makes 4 servings

6 slices bacon, chopped

1 large shallot or small onion, finely chopped

1 serrano or jalapeño pepper, minced

3½ cups chicken broth

1 cup uncooked grits*

½ teaspoon salt

¼ teaspoon black pepper

1 cup (4 ounces) shredded Cheddar cheese

½ cup half-and-half

2 tablespoons finely chopped green onion

Do not use instant grits.

1 Press Sauté; cook bacon in Instant Pot until crisp. Drain on paper towel-lined plate. Drain off all but 1 tablespoon drippings.

2 Add shallot and serrano pepper to pot; cook and stir 2 minutes or until shallot is lightly browned. Add broth, grits, salt and black pepper; cook and stir 1 minute.

3 Secure lid and move pressure release valve to Sealing position. Press Pressure Cook or Manual; cook at high pressure 14 minutes.

4 When cooking is complete, use natural release for 10 minutes, then release remaining pressure.

5 Stir grits until smooth. Add cheese, half-and-half and half of bacon; stir until well blended. Sprinkle with green onion and remaining bacon.

Lentil Bolognese

Makes 6 servings

2 tablespoons olive oil

1 onion, chopped

1 carrot, chopped

1 stalk celery, chopped

2 cloves garlic, minced

1 teaspoon salt

½ teaspoon dried oregano

   Pinch red pepper flakes

3 tablespoons tomato paste

¼ cup dry white wine

3¼ cups water or vegetable broth

1 can (28 ounces) crushed tomatoes

1 can (about 14 ounces) diced tomatoes

1 cup dried lentils, rinsed and sorted

1 portobello mushroom, gills removed, finely chopped

2 cups uncooked whole wheat rotini pasta

1 Press Sauté; heat oil in Instant Pot. Add onion, carrot and celery; cook and stir 7 minutes or until onion is lightly browned and carrot is softened.

2 Stir in garlic, salt, oregano and red pepper flakes. Add tomato paste; cook and stir 1 minute. Add wine; cook and stir until absorbed. Stir in water, crushed tomatoes, diced tomatoes, lentils and mushroom; mix well.

3 Secure lid and move pressure release valve to Sealing position. Press Pressure Cook or Manual; cook at high pressure 5 minutes. When cooking is complete, use quick release.

4 Stir in pasta. Secure lid and move pressure release valve to Sealing position. Press Pressure Cook or Manual; cook at high pressure 4 minutes. When cooking is complete, use quick release.

Mushroom Risotto

Makes 4 servings

2 tablespoons olive oil

¾ cup chopped shallots *or* 1 small onion, chopped

8 ounces sliced mushrooms

3 cloves garlic, minced

1½ cups uncooked arborio rice

¼ cup Madeira wine

3½ cups vegetable broth

½ teaspoon salt

¼ teaspoon black pepper

⅔ cup grated Romano cheese

3 tablespoons chopped fresh parsley

2 tablespoons butter

1 Press Sauté; heat oil in Instant Pot. Add shallots; cook and stir 2 minutes or until softened. Add mushrooms; cook and stir about 6 minutes or until liquid evaporates and mushrooms begin to brown. Add garlic; cook and stir 30 seconds. Add rice; cook and stir 1 minute. Add Madeira; cook and stir 1 minute or until almost evaporated. Stir in broth, salt and pepper; mix well.

2 Secure lid and move pressure release valve to Sealing position. Press Pressure Cook or Manual; cook at high pressure 6 minutes.

3 When cooking is complete, use quick release.

4 Press Sauté; adjust heat to low. Cook about 3 minutes or until risotto reaches desired consistency, stirring constantly. Stir in cheese, parsley and butter until blended.

Chickpea Tikka Masala

Makes 4 servings

1¼ cups dried chickpeas,
  soaked 8 hours
  or overnight
1 tablespoon olive oil
1 onion, chopped
3 cloves garlic, minced
1 tablespoon minced fresh
  ginger or ginger paste
1 tablespoon garam masala
1½ teaspoons salt
1 teaspoon ground coriander
1 teaspoon ground cumin
¼ teaspoon ground
  red pepper
1 can (28 ounces)
  crushed tomatoes
1 can (about 13 ounces)
  coconut milk
1 package (about 12 ounces)
  paneer cheese, cut
  into 1-inch cubes
  Hot cooked basmati rice
  (optional)
  Chopped fresh cilantro

1 Drain and rinse chickpeas. Press Sauté; heat oil in Instant Pot. Add onion; cook and stir 5 minutes or until translucent. Add garlic, ginger, garam masala, salt, coriander, cumin and red pepper; cook and stir 1 minute. Stir in chickpeas, tomatoes and coconut milk; mix well.

2 Secure lid and move pressure release valve to Sealing position. Press Pressure Cook or Manual; cook at high pressure 22 minutes.

3 When cooking is complete, use natural release for 10 minutes, then release remaining pressure.

4 Press Sauté; adjust heat to low. Add paneer to pot; stir gently. Cook 5 minutes or until paneer is heated through, stirring occasionally. Serve with rice, if desired; garnish with cilantro.

Variation

For a vegan dish, substitute 1 package (about 12 ounces) firm silken tofu, drained and cut into 1-inch cubes, for the paneer.

Southwestern Mac and Cheese

Makes 6 to 8 servings

4 tablespoons (½ stick) butter, divided

1 onion, finely chopped

3⅓ cups water

1 package (16 ounces) uncooked elbow macaroni

1 can (about 14 ounces) diced tomatoes with green peppers and onions

1 teaspoon salt

4 cups (16 ounces) shredded Mexican cheese blend, divided

½ cup milk

1 cup salsa

1 Press Sauté; melt 1 tablespoon butter in Instant Pot. Add onion; cook and stir 3 minutes or until softened. Stir in water, macaroni, tomatoes and salt; mix well.

2 Secure lid and move pressure release valve to Sealing position. Press Pressure Cook or Manual; cook at high pressure 4 minutes.

3 When cooking is complete, use quick release.

4 Press Sauté; add 3½ cups cheese, milk and remaining 3 tablespoons butter to pot. Stir until smooth and well blended. Stir in salsa. Press Cancel. Sprinkle remaining ½ cup cheese over pasta; cover and let stand until melted.

Vegetarian Chili
Makes 8 servings

2 tablespoons olive oil

1 onion, finely chopped

2 medium carrots, chopped

1 red bell pepper, chopped

3 tablespoons chili powder

2 tablespoons tomato paste

2 tablespoons packed
   dark brown sugar

2 tablespoons ground cumin

3 cloves garlic, minced

1 tablespoon dried oregano

2 teaspoons salt

1 can (28 ounces)
   diced tomatoes

1 can (15 ounces)
   tomato sauce

1 can (about 15 ounces)
   small white beans,
   rinsed and drained

1 can (about 15 ounces)
   light kidney beans,
   rinsed and drained

1 can (about 15 ounces)
   dark kidney beans,
   rinsed and drained

1 can (about 15 ounces) pinto
   beans, rinsed and drained

1 can (4 ounces) diced
   green chiles

1 ounce unsweetened
   chocolate, chopped

1 tablespoon cider vinegar

1 Press Sauté; heat oil in Instant Pot. Add onion, carrots and bell pepper; cook and stir 5 minutes or until vegetables are softened. Add chili powder, tomato paste, brown sugar, cumin, garlic, oregano and salt; cook and stir 1 minute. Stir in tomatoes, tomato sauce, beans and chiles; mix well.

2 Secure lid and move pressure release valve to Sealing position. Press Pressure Cook or Manual; cook at high pressure 10 minutes.

3 When cooking is complete, use natural release for 10 minutes, then release remaining pressure. Stir in chocolate and vinegar until blended.

Mushroom and Chickpea Ragoût

Makes 6 servings

1 cup dried chickpeas, soaked 8 hours or overnight

3 tablespoons extra virgin olive oil

8 ounces sliced cremini mushrooms

8 ounces shiitake mushrooms,* stemmed and thinly sliced

1 onion, chopped

4 cloves garlic, minced

½ cup Madeira wine

2 teaspoons salt

1 teaspoon dried rosemary

Black pepper

1 can (28 ounces) crushed tomatoes

1 cup water

1 can (6 ounces) tomato paste

Polenta (recipe follows)

Or substitute an additional 8 ounces of cremini mushrooms for the shiitake mushrooms.

1 Drain and rinse chickpeas. Press Sauté; heat oil in Instant Pot. Add mushrooms, onion and garlic; cook and stir 6 to 8 minutes or until mushrooms are browned. Add Madeira, salt and rosemary; cook and stir 1 to 2 minutes or until liquid is almost evaporated. Season with pepper. Stir in chickpeas, tomatoes, water and tomato paste; mix well.

2 Secure lid and move pressure release valve to Sealing position. Press Pressure Cook or Manual; cook at high pressure 22 minutes.

3 When cooking is complete, use natural release for 10 minutes, then release remaining pressure. Meanwhile, prepare Polenta.

4 Stir ragoût; serve over Polenta.

Polenta

Combine 2 cups milk, 2 cups water and ¼ teaspoon salt in large saucepan; bring to a boil over medium-high heat. Slowly whisk in 1 cup instant polenta in thin, steady stream. Cook 4 to 5 minutes or until thick and creamy, whisking constantly. Remove from heat; stir in ½ cup grated Parmesan cheese.

Pumpkin Risotto

Makes 4 servings

2 tablespoons butter

1 tablespoon olive oil

1 onion, finely chopped

2 cloves garlic, minced

1½ cups uncooked arborio rice

1 teaspoon salt

¼ teaspoon ground nutmeg

⅛ teaspoon black pepper

½ cup dry white wine

4 cups vegetable broth

1 can (15 ounces) pure pumpkin

5 fresh sage leaves

½ cup shredded Parmesan cheese, plus additional for serving

¼ cup roasted pumpkin seeds (pepitas)

1 Press Sauté; heat butter and oil in Instant Pot. Add onion and garlic; cook and stir 3 minutes or until softened. Add rice; cook and stir 4 minutes or until rice is translucent. Stir in salt, nutmeg and pepper. Add wine; cook and stir about 1 minute or until evaporated. Stir in broth, pumpkin and sage; mix well.

2 Secure lid and move pressure release valve to Sealing position. Press Pressure Cook or Manual; cook at high pressure 6 minutes.

3 When cooking is complete, use quick release.

4 Press Sauté; adjust heat to low. Cook about 3 minutes or until risotto reaches desired consistency, stirring constantly. Stir in ½ cup cheese until blended. Serve immediately with additional cheese and pumpkin seeds.

Sweet Potato and Black Bean Chili

Makes 6 servings

1 tablespoon olive oil

1 large onion, chopped

4 teaspoons chili powder

2 cloves garlic, minced

1 teaspoon salt

1 teaspoon chipotle chili powder

½ teaspoon ground cumin

2 cans (about 15 ounces each) black beans, rinsed and drained

1 large sweet potato, peeled and cut into ½-inch pieces

1 can (about 14 ounces) diced tomatoes

1 can (about 14 ounces) crushed tomatoes

1½ cups vegetable broth or water

Optional toppings: sour cream, sliced green onions, shredded Cheddar cheese and/or tortilla chips

1 Press Sauté; heat oil in Instant Pot. Add onion; cook and stir 3 minutes or until softened. Add chili powder, garlic, salt, chipotle chili powder and cumin; cook and stir 1 minute. Add beans, sweet potato, diced tomatoes, crushed tomatoes and broth; mix well.

2 Secure lid and move pressure release valve to Sealing position. Press Pressure Cook or Manual; cook at high pressure 4 minutes.

3 When cooking is complete, use quick release.

4 Press Sauté; cook and stir 3 to 5 minutes or until chili thickens to desired consistency. Serve with desired toppings.

Classic Hummus
Makes about 3¼ cups

4 cups water

8 ounces dried chickpeas, rinsed and sorted

1½ teaspoons salt, divided

¼ cup lemon juice

2 cloves garlic, minced

¼ teaspoon ground cumin

½ cup tahini

2 tablespoons extra virgin olive oil, plus additional for serving

Chopped fresh parsley (optional)

Zaatar or paprika (optional)

1 Combine water, chickpeas and 1 teaspoon salt in Instant Pot. Secure lid and move pressure release valve to Sealing position. Press Pressure Cook or Manual; cook at high pressure 45 minutes.

2 When cooking is complete, use natural release. Drain chickpeas, reserving 1 cup cooking liquid.

3 Combine lemon juice, garlic, remaining ½ teaspoon salt and cumin in bowl of food processor; let stand 5 minutes. Add tahini and ¼ cup cooking liquid; process until well blended. Add cooked chickpeas, 2 tablespoons oil and ⅓ cup cooking liquid; process about 3 minutes or until very smooth, stopping to scrape down side of bowl once or twice. Add additional cooking liquid, 1 tablespoon at a time, if necessary to thin hummus.

4 Top with additional oil, parsley and zaatar or paprika, if desired.

Barley with Asparagus and Peas
Makes 6 servings

2 tablespoons olive oil, divided

1 pound asparagus, cut diagonally into 1½-inch pieces

2 shallots *or* 1 small onion, finely chopped, divided

1 clove garlic, minced

1½ cups uncooked pearl barley

2 cups vegetable broth

Grated peel and juice of 1 lemon, divided

1 teaspoon salt

¼ teaspoon black pepper

1 cup thawed frozen peas

½ cup grated Parmesan cheese, divided (optional)

2 green onions, chopped

1 Press Sauté; heat 1 tablespoon oil in Instant Pot. Add asparagus and 1 shallot; cook and stir 5 minutes or until asparagus is crisp-tender. Remove to small bowl. Add remaining 1 tablespoon oil, 1 shallot and garlic to pot; cook and stir 1 minute. Add barley; cook and stir 2 minutes. Stir in broth, lemon peel, half of lemon juice, salt and pepper; mix well.

2 Secure lid and move pressure release valve to Sealing position. Cook at high pressure 21 minutes.

3 When cooking is complete, use natural release for 10 minutes, then release remaining pressure.

4 Press Sauté; stir in asparagus, peas, half of cheese, if desired, remaining lemon juice and green onions. Cook 2 minutes or until heated through, stirring occasionally. Serve with remaining cheese.

Greek Rice
Makes 6 to 8 servings

1¾ cups uncooked long grain rice

2 tablespoons butter

1¾ cups vegetable or chicken broth

1 teaspoon Greek seasoning

1 teaspoon dried oregano

¼ teaspoon salt

1 cup pitted kalamata olives, drained and chopped

¾ cup chopped roasted red peppers

Crumbled feta cheese (optional)

Chopped fresh Italian parsley (optional)

1 Rinse rice well; drain in fine-mesh strainer.

2 Press Sauté; melt butter in Instant Pot. Add rice; cook 5 to 6 minutes or until golden brown, stirring occasionally. Add broth, Greek seasoning, oregano and salt; mix well.

3 Secure lid and move pressure release valve to Sealing position. Press Pressure Cook or Manual; cook at high pressure 4 minutes.

4 When cooking is complete, use natural release for 10 minutes, then release remaining pressure.

5 Stir in olives and roasted peppers; garnish with cheese and parsley.

Cheesy Polenta
Makes 6 servings

5 cups vegetable broth

½ teaspoon salt

1½ cups uncooked instant polenta

½ cup grated Parmesan cheese

¼ cup (½ stick) butter, cubed, plus additional for serving

Fried sage leaves (optional)

1 Combine broth and salt in Instant Pot; slowly whisk in polenta until blended.

2 Secure lid and move pressure release valve to Sealing position. Press Pressure Cook or Manual; cook at high pressure 5 minutes.

3 When cooking is complete, use natural release for 5 minutes, then release remaining pressure.

4 Whisk in cheese and ¼ cup butter until well blended. (Polenta may appear separated immediately after cooking but will come together when stirred.) Serve with additional butter; garnish with sage.

Tip

Spread any leftover polenta in a baking dish and refrigerate until cold. Cut the cold polenta into sticks or slices, brush with olive oil and pan-fry or grill until lightly browned.

Note

Chicken broth may be substituted for vegetable broth. Or use water and add an additional ½ teaspoon salt when whisking in the polenta.

VEGETABLES

Garlic Parmesan Spaghetti Squash
Makes 2 servings

- 1 medium spaghetti squash (2 to 2½ pounds)
- 1 cup water
- 2 tablespoons extra virgin olive oil
- 1 clove garlic, minced
- ¼ teaspoon salt
- ¼ teaspoon red pepper flakes
- ⅛ teaspoon black pepper
- ½ cup shredded Parmesan cheese
- ⅓ cup chopped fresh parsley

1 Cut squash in half; remove and discard seeds. Pour water into Instant Pot; place rack in pot. Place squash halves on rack cut sides up.

2 Secure lid and move pressure release valve to Sealing position. Press Pressure Cook or Manual; cook at high pressure 7 minutes.

3 When cooking is complete, use quick release. Remove squash to plate; let stand until cool enough to handle. Use fork to shred squash into long strands, reserving shells for serving, if desired.

4 Pour out cooking water and dry pot with paper towel. Press Sauté; adjust heat to low. Add oil, garlic, salt, red pepper flakes and black pepper to pot; cook and stir 2 minutes or until garlic begins to turn golden. Press Cancel. Add squash, cheese and parsley; cook and stir gently just until blended. Serve immediately.

Beet and Arugula Salad

Makes 6 to 8 servings

1 cup water

8 medium beets
(5 to 6 ounces each)

⅓ cup red wine vinegar

¾ teaspoon salt

½ teaspoon black pepper

3 tablespoons extra virgin
olive oil

1 package (about 5 ounces)
baby arugula

1 package (4 ounces)
goat cheese with garlic
and herbs, crumbled

1 Pour water into Instant Pot; place rack in pot. Arrange beets on rack (or use steamer basket to hold beets). Secure lid and move pressure release valve to Sealing position. Press Pressure Cook or Manual; cook at high pressure 20 minutes.

2 When cooking is complete, use natural release for 10 minutes, then release remaining pressure. Set beets aside until cool enough to handle.

3 Meanwhile, whisk vinegar, salt and pepper in large bowl. Slowly add oil in thin, steady stream, whisking until well blended. Remove 3 tablespoons dressing to medium bowl.

4 Peel beets and cut into wedges. Add warm beets to large bowl; toss to coat with dressing. Add arugula to medium bowl; toss gently to coat with dressing. Place arugula on platter or plates, top with beets and cheese.

Warm Potato Salad

Makes 6 to 8 servings

2 pounds upeeled fingerling potatoes

³/₄ cup water

3 slices thick-cut bacon, cut into ½-inch pieces

1 small onion, diced

2 tablespoons olive oil

¼ cup cider vinegar

2 tablespoons capers, drained

1 tablespoon Dijon mustard

³/₄ teaspoon salt

¼ teaspoon black pepper

¹/₃ cup chopped fresh parsley

1 Combine potatoes and water in Instant Pot. Secure lid and move pressure release valve to Sealing position. Press Pressure Cook or Manual; cook at high pressure 4 minutes.

2 When cooking is complete, use quick release. Drain potatoes; let stand until cool enough to handle. Dry out pot with paper towel.

3 Press Sauté; cook bacon in pot until crisp. Drain on paper towel-lined plate. Drain off all but 1 tablespoon drippings from pot. Adjust heat to low. Add onion and oil to pot; cook about 10 minutes or until onion begins to turn golden, stirring occasionally. Meanwhile, cut potatoes crosswise into ½-inch slices.

4 Add vinegar, capers, mustard, salt and pepper to pot; mix well. Turn off heat; stir in potatoes. Add parsley and bacon; stir gently to coat.

Faster Collard Greens

Makes 4 to 6 servings

4 slices thick-cut bacon,
    cut into ½-inch pieces

1 pound collard greens,
    stems trimmed,
    roughly chopped

½ cup water or chicken broth

1 tablespoon cider vinegar

1 tablespoon packed
    brown sugar

¼ teaspoon salt

¼ teaspoon black pepper

¼ teaspoon red pepper flakes

1 Press Sauté; cook bacon in Instant Pot until crisp. Add half of greens; cook 1 minute or until greens begin to wilt, scraping up browned bits from bottom of pot. Add remaining greens; cook and stir 1 minute. Stir in water, vinegar, brown sugar, salt, black pepper and red pepper flakes; mix well.

2 Secure lid and move pressure release valve to Sealing position. Press Pressure Cook or Manual; cook at high pressure 20 minutes.

3 When cooking is complete, use quick release. Stir greens; serve warm.

Mashed Sweet Potatoes and Parsnips

Makes 6 servings

2 large sweet potatoes (about 1½ pounds), peeled and cut into 1-inch pieces

2 medium parsnips (about 12 ounces), peeled and cut into ½-inch slices

½ cup water

1 teaspoon salt

¼ cup evaporated milk

2 tablespoons butter

⅛ teaspoon ground nutmeg

¼ cup chopped fresh chives or green onions

1 Combine sweet potatoes, parsnips, water and salt in Instant Pot. Secure lid and move pressure release valve to Sealing position. Press Pressure Cook or Manual; cook at high pressure 10 minutes.

2 When cooking is complete, use quick release.

3 Add milk, butter and nutmeg to pot; mash with potato masher until smooth. Stir in chives.

Baba Ganoush

Makes about 2½ cups

1½ tablespoons olive oil, divided, plus additional for serving

1½ tablespoons dark sesame oil, divided

2 medium eggplants (about 1 pound each), peeled and cut in half lengthwise

½ cup water

1 clove garlic, minced

¼ cup tahini

2 tablespoons lemon juice

1 teaspoon salt

¼ teaspoon black pepper

Chopped fresh parsley

1 Press Sauté; heat half of olive oil and half of sesame oil in Instant Pot. Add two eggplant halves, cut sides down; cook about 5 minutes or until well browned. Remove to plate. Repeat with remaining oil and eggplant halves.

2 Return all eggplant to pot; add water and garlic. Secure lid and move pressure release valve to Sealing position. Press Pressure Cook or Manual; cook at high pressure 8 minutes.

3 When cooking is complete, use quick release. Drain eggplant in colander 5 minutes.

4 Transfer eggplant to medium bowl; mash with potato masher until no large pieces remain.* Add tahini, lemon juice, salt and pepper; stir until well blended. Garnish with parsley and additional olive oil.

For a smoother dip, transfer cooked eggplant to food processor with tahini, lemon juice, salt and pepper; process until smooth.

Quick-Cooking Ratatouille

Makes about 6 cups

2 tablespoons extra virgin olive oil

1 medium onion, chopped

2 red bell peppers, cut into 1-inch pieces

3 cloves garlic, minced

1 teaspoon Italian seasoning

Pinch red pepper flakes

1 can (28 ounces) whole tomatoes, undrained, coarsely chopped or crushed with hands

1 medium eggplant (about 1 pound), cut into ½-inch pieces

3 small zucchini (about 12 ounces), cut in half lengthwise and cut crosswise into ¾-inch slices

1 large sprig fresh basil

1 tablespoon tomato paste

1½ teaspoons salt

¼ teaspoon black pepper

1 tablespoon balsamic or red wine vinegar

¼ cup chopped fresh basil

1 Press Sauté; heat oil in Instant Pot. Add onion; cook and stir 2 minutes. Add bell peppers; cook and stir 3 minutes. Add garlic, Italian seasoning and red pepper flakes; cook and stir 30 seconds.

2 Stir in tomatoes with juice, eggplant, zucchini, basil sprig, tomato paste, salt and black pepper; mix well. Secure lid and move pressure release valve to Sealing position. Press Pressure Cook or Manual; cook at high pressure 1 minute.

3 When cooking is complete, use quick release. Press Sauté; cook about 5 minutes or until slightly thickened. Remove and discard basil sprig. Stir in vinegar and chopped basil. Serve warm or at room temperature.

Cauliflower and Potato Masala

Makes 6 servings

1 tablespoon olive or
   vegetable oil

2 teaspoons minced garlic

1 teaspoon minced
   fresh ginger

1 teaspoon salt

1 teaspoon cumin seeds
   or ½ teaspoon ground
   cumin

1 teaspoon ground coriander

1 teaspoon garam masala

1 can (about 14 ounces)
   diced tomatoes

1 head cauliflower (about
   1¼ pounds), broken
   into florets

1 pound red potatoes
   (2 large), peeled and
   cut into ½-inch wedges

2 tablespoons chopped
   fresh cilantro

1 Press Sauté; heat oil in Instant Pot. Add garlic, ginger, salt, cumin, coriander and garam masala; cook and stir about 30 seconds or until fragrant. Add tomatoes; cook and stir 1 minute. Add cauliflower and potatoes; mix well.

2 Secure lid and move pressure release valve to Sealing position. Press Pressure Cook or Manual; cook at high pressure 2 minutes.

3 When cooking is complete, use quick release. Sprinkle with cilantro.

Brussels Sprouts in Orange Sauce

Makes 4 servings

½ cup plus 2 tablespoons orange juice, divided

½ teaspoon salt

¼ teaspoon red pepper flakes

¼ teaspoon ground cinnamon

¼ teaspoon black pepper

8 ounces fresh brussels sprouts (about 3 cups)

2 teaspoons cornstarch

1 teaspoon honey

1 teaspoon shredded or grated orange peel

1 Combine ½ cup orange juice, salt, red pepper flakes, cinnamon and black pepper in Instant Pot; mix well. Stir in brussels sprouts.

2 Secure lid and move pressure release valve to Sealing position. Press Pressure Cook or Manual; cook at high pressure 2 minutes.

3 When cooking is complete, use quick release. Remove brussels sprouts to medium bowl with slotted spoon.

4 Stir remaining 2 tablespoons orange juice into cornstarch in small bowl until smooth. Press Sauté; add honey, orange peel and cornstarch mixture to pot. Cook 1 to 2 minutes or until sauce thickens, stirring constantly. Pour sauce over brussels sprouts; stir gently to coat.

Caribbean Sweet Potatoes

Makes 6 to 8 servings

2½ pounds sweet potatoes, peeled and cut into 1-inch pieces

8 ounces shredded peeled carrots

¾ cup flaked coconut, divided

½ cup water

¼ cup (½ stick) butter, cut into pieces

2 tablespoons sugar

1 teaspoon salt

½ cup chopped walnuts, toasted*

2 tablespoons lime juice

1 teaspoon grated lime peel

To toast walnuts, cook in small skillet over medium heat 6 to 8 minutes or until fragrant, stirring frequently.

1 Combine sweet potatoes, carrots, ½ cup coconut, water, butter, sugar and salt in Instant Pot; mix well.

2 Secure lid and move pressure release valve to Sealing position. Press Pressure Cook or Manual; cook at high pressure 5 minutes. Meanwhile, place remaining ¼ cup coconut in small skillet; cook 4 minutes or until lightly browned, stirring frequently.

3 When cooking is complete, use quick release.

4 Mash sweet potatoes in pot until desired consistency. Stir in walnuts, lime juice and lime peel until blended. Sprinkle with toasted coconut.

Eggplant Italiano

Makes 6 servings

- 1 tablespoon olive oil
- 2 medium onions, thinly sliced
- 1¼ pounds eggplant, cut into 1-inch cubes
- 2 stalks celery, cut into 1-inch pieces
- 1 can (about 14 ounces) diced tomatoes
- ½ cup pitted black olives, sliced
- 3 tablespoons tomato sauce
- 2 tablespoons balsamic vinegar
- 1 tablespoon sugar
- 1 tablespoon capers, drained
- 1 teaspoon dried oregano or basil
- ¾ teaspoon salt
- ¼ teaspoon black pepper

1 Press Sauté; heat oil in Instant Pot. Add onions; cook and stir 3 minutes or until softened. Add eggplant, celery, tomatoes, olives, tomato sauce, vinegar, sugar, capers, oregano, salt and pepper; mix well.

2 Secure lid and move pressure release valve to Sealing position. Press Pressure Cook or Manual; cook at high pressure 2 minutes.

3 When cooking is complete, use quick release.

Thai Red Curry with Tofu

Makes 4 servings

- 2 tablespoons vegetable oil
- 5 medium shallots, thinly sliced (about 1½ cups)
- 3 tablespoons Thai red curry paste
- 1 teaspoon minced garlic
- 1 teaspoon grated fresh ginger
- 1 can (about 13 ounces) unsweetened coconut milk
- 1 medium sweet potato, peeled and cut into 1-inch pieces
- 1 small eggplant or large zucchini, halved lengthwise and cut crosswise into ½-inch slices
- 1½ tablespoons soy sauce
- 1 tablespoon packed brown sugar
- 1 package (14 to 16 ounces) extra firm tofu, cut into 1-inch pieces
- 1 red bell pepper, cut into ¼-inch strips
- ½ cup green beans (1-inch pieces)
- ¼ cup chopped fresh basil
- 2 tablespoons lime juice
- Hot cooked rice (optional)

1 Press Sauté; heat oil in Instant Pot. Add shallots; cook and stir 2 minutes or until softened. Add curry paste, garlic and ginger; cook and stir 1 minute. Stir in coconut milk, sweet potato, eggplant, soy sauce and brown sugar; mix well.

2 Secure lid and move pressure release valve to Sealing position. Press Pressure Cook or Manual; cook at high pressure 4 minutes.

3 When cooking is complete, use quick release. Add tofu, bell pepper and green beans to pot. Secure lid and move pressure release valve to Sealing position. Press Pressure Cook or Manual; cook at low pressure 1 minute.

4 When cooking is complete, use quick release. Stir in basil and lime juice. Serve with rice, if desired.

Chunky Ranch Potatoes

Makes 8 servings

3 pounds unpeeled red potatoes, quartered

½ cup water

1 teaspoon salt

½ cup ranch dressing

½ cup grated Parmesan cheese

¼ cup minced fresh chives

1 Combine potatoes, water and salt in Instant Pot; mix well.

2 Secure lid and move pressure release valve to Sealing position. Press Pressure Cook or Manual; cook at high pressure 5 minutes.

3 When cooking is complete, use quick release.

4 Add ranch dressing, cheese and chives to pot; stir gently to coat, breaking potatoes into chunks.

Sweet and Sour Red Cabbage

Makes 8 servings

- 2 slices thick-cut bacon, chopped
- 1 cup chopped onion
- 1 head red cabbage (2 to 3 pounds), thinly sliced (about 8 cups)
- 1 pound unpeeled Granny Smith apples, cut into ½-inch pieces (about 2 medium)
- ½ cup honey
- ½ cup cider vinegar
- ¼ cup plus 3 tablespoons water, divided
- 1 teaspoon salt
- 1 teaspoon celery salt
- ¼ teaspoon black pepper
- 2 tablespoons all-purpose flour

1 Press Sauté, cook bacon in Instant Pot until crisp. Remove to paper towel-lined plate.

2 Add onion to pot; cook and stir 3 minutes or until softened. Stir in cabbage, apples, honey, vinegar, ¼ cup water, salt, celery salt and pepper; mix well.

3 Secure lid and move pressure release valve to Sealing position. Press Pressure Cook or Manual; cook at high pressure 5 minutes.

4 When cooking is complete, use natural release for 10 minutes, then release remaining pressure.

5 Stir remaining 3 tablespoons water into flour in small bowl until smooth. Press Sauté; add flour mixture to pot. Cook and stir about 3 minutes or until sauce thickens. Sprinkle with bacon; serve warm.

Corn and Sweet Potato Curry

Makes 6 servings

1 tablespoon vegetable oil

1 large onion, chopped

2 tablespoons minced
   fresh ginger

½ jalapeño pepper,
   seeded and minced

2 cloves garlic, minced

1 cup frozen corn

2 teaspoons curry powder

½ teaspoon salt

1 can (about 13 ounces)
   coconut milk, well shaken

1 tablespoon soy sauce

4 sweet potatoes,
   peeled and cut
   into ¾-inch pieces

Hot cooked jasmine
   or long grain rice

Optional toppings:
   chopped fresh cilantro,
   finely chopped green
   onions, chopped roasted
   peanuts

1 Press Sauté; heat oil in Instant Pot. Add onion, ginger, jalapeño and garlic; cook and stir 3 minutes or until softened. Add corn, curry powder and salt; cook and stir 1 minute. Add coconut milk and soy sauce; stir until well blended. Stir in sweet potatoes; mix well.

2 Secure lid and move pressure release valve to Sealing position. Press Pressure Cook or Manual; cook at high pressure 3 minutes.

3 When cooking is complete, use quick release.

4 Press Sauté; cook about 2 minutes or until sauce thickens to desired consistency. Serve over rice; garnish as desired.

Spicy Asian Green Beans

Makes 4 servings

1 cup water

1 pound fresh green beans, trimmed

2 tablespoons chopped green onions

2 tablespoons dry sherry or chicken broth

1½ tablespoons reduced-sodium soy sauce

1 teaspoon chili sauce with garlic

1 teaspoon dark sesame oil

1 clove garlic, minced

1 Pour water into Instant Pot; place rack in pot. Place beans on rack. (Arrange beans perpendicular to rack to prevent beans from falling through.)

2 Secure lid and move pressure release valve to Sealing position. Press Pressure Cook or Manual; cook at high pressure 2 minutes.

3 When cooking is complete, use quick release. Remove rack from pot; drain off and discard cooking liquid. Place beans in large bowl.

4 Press Sauté; add green onions, sherry, soy sauce, chili sauce, oil and garlic to pot. Cook and stir 1 to 2 minutes or until heated through. Pour sauce over beans; toss to coat.

Mashed Root Vegetables

Makes 6 servings

1 pound baking potatoes, peeled and cut into 1-inch pieces

1 pound turnips, peeled and cut into 1-inch pieces

12 ounces sweet potatoes, peeled and cut into 1-inch pieces

8 ounces parsnips, peeled and cut into ½-inch pieces

¼ cup (½ stick) butter, cubed

⅓ cup water

2 teaspoons salt

¼ teaspoon black pepper

½ cup milk

1 Combine baking potatoes, turnips, sweet potatoes, parsnips, butter, water, salt and pepper in Instant Pot; mix well.

2 Secure lid and move pressure release valve to Sealing position. Press Pressure Cook or Manual; cook at high pressure 10 minutes.

3 When cooking is complete, use quick release.

4 Mash vegetables with potato masher until almost smooth. Press Sauté; stir in milk until blended. Cook and stir about 3 minutes or until milk is absorbed and vegetables reach desired consistency.

Orange-Spiced Glazed Carrots

Makes 6 servings

1 package (32 ounces)
   baby carrots

½ cup orange juice

⅓ cup packed brown sugar

3 tablespoons butter,
   cut into pieces

¾ teaspoon ground cinnamon

½ teaspoon salt

¼ teaspoon ground nutmeg

¼ cup water

2 tablespoons cornstarch

Grated orange peel
   (optional)

Chopped fresh parsley
   (optional)

1 Combine carrots, orange juice, brown sugar, butter, cinnamon, salt and nutmeg in Instant Pot; mix well.

2 Secure lid and move pressure release valve to Sealing position. Press Pressure Cook or Manual; cook at high pressure 2 minutes.

3 When cooking is complete, use quick release.

4 Stir water into cornstarch in small bowl until smooth. Press Sauté; add cornstarch mixture to pot. Cook and stir 1 to 2 minutes or until sauce thickens. Garnish with orange peel and parsley.

Quick Vegetable Curry

Makes 6 to 8 servings

2 teaspoons salt

2 teaspoons curry powder

1 teaspoon cumin seeds

1 teaspoon ground coriander

¼ teaspoon ground turmeric

¼ teaspoon ground red pepper

1 tablespoon vegetable oil

1 large onion, finely chopped

4 cloves garlic, minced

1 tablespoon grated fresh ginger

¼ cup tomato paste

1 cup water

1 head cauliflower (about 1 pound), broken into florets

2 baking potatoes, peeled and cut into ½-inch pieces

1 red bell pepper, cut into ½-inch pieces

2 carrots, cut into ¼-inch pieces

1 package (12 ounces) frozen peas, thawed

1 Combine salt, curry powder, cumin, coriander, turmeric and ground red pepper in small bowl; mix well.

2 Press Sauté; heat oil in Instant Pot. Add onion; cook and stir 3 minutes or until softened. Add garlic, ginger and spice mixture; cook and stir 1 minute. Add tomato paste; cook and stir 30 seconds. Stir in water, scraping up browned bits from bottom of pot. Add cauliflower, potatoes, bell pepper and carrots; stir to coat with sauce.

3 Secure lid and move pressure release valve to Sealing position. Press Pressure Cook or Manual; cook at high pressure 2 minutes.

4 When cooking is complete, use quick release. Stir in peas; cover and let stand 2 to 3 minutes or until heated through.

DESSERTS

Big Chocolate Chip Cookie
Makes 6 to 8 servings

1 cup plus 2 tablespoons all-purpose flour

½ teaspoon baking soda

½ teaspoon salt

¼ cup (½ stick) butter, softened

½ cup packed brown sugar

2 tablespoons granulated sugar

1 egg

½ teaspoon vanilla

1 cup semisweet chocolate chunks or chips

1 cup water

Vanilla ice cream (optional)

1 Spray 7-inch metal cake pan with nonstick cooking spray. Combine flour, baking soda and salt in small bowl; mix well.

2 Beat butter, brown sugar and granulated sugar in medium bowl with electric mixer at medium speed until light and creamy. Add egg and vanilla; beat until well blended. Add flour mixture; beat just until blended. Stir in chocolate chunks. Spread batter in prepared pan. Cover pan with paper towel (to absorb moisture), making sure paper towel does not touch batter. Cover pan with foil over paper towel.

3 Pour water into Instant Pot; place rack in pot. Place pan on rack. Secure lid and move pressure release valve to Sealing position. Press Pressure Cook or Manual; cook at high pressure 35 minutes.

4 When cooking is complete, use natural release 10 minutes, then release remaining pressure. Remove pan from pot. Uncover; cool on wire rack 15 minutes. Invert cookie onto plate; invert again onto serving plate. Serve warm or at room temperature with ice cream, if desired.

Brioche Rum Custard

Makes 4 to 6 servings

1¾ cups whipping cream

2 eggs

⅓ cup packed dark brown sugar

3 tablespoons light rum

1 teaspoon vanilla

¼ teaspoon salt

1 loaf (10 to 12 ounces) brioche bread or challah, torn into pieces

½ cup chopped pecans, divided

1¼ cups water

Caramel or butterscotch ice cream topping (optional)

1 Spray 6- to 7-inch (1½-quart) soufflé dish or round baking dish with nonstick cooking spray.

2 Whisk cream, eggs, brown sugar, rum, vanilla and salt in large bowl until well blended. Add brioche and ¼ cup pecans; stir until blended, Pour into prepared soufflé dish; sprinkle with remaining ¼ cup pecans. Cover dish with foil.

3 Pour water into Instant Pot; place rack in pot. Place soufflé dish on rack. Secure lid and move pressure release valve to Sealing position. Press Pressure Cook or Manual; cook at high pressure 35 minutes.

4 When cooking is complete, use natural release for 10 minutes, then release remaining pressure. Remove soufflé dish from pot. Uncover; serve warm or at room temperature. Drizzle with caramel topping, if desired.

Chocolate Truffle Cake

Makes 8 servings

Unsweetened cocoa
powder

12 ounces bittersweet (60%)
chocolate, chopped

½ cup (1 stick) butter, cut
into pieces

5 eggs, separated

1 teaspoon vanilla

¼ teaspoon salt

½ cup granulated sugar

1½ cups water

Powdered sugar and fresh
raspberries (optional)

1 Spray 7-inch springform pan with nonstick cooking spray; dust with cocoa powder.

2 Combine chocolate and butter in large microwavable bowl; microwave on MEDIUM (50%) 2 minutes or until melted and smooth, stirring after each minute. Set aside to cool 5 minutes. Beat egg yolks and vanilla into chocolate mixture until well blended.

3 Beat egg whites and salt in medium bowl with electric mixer at medium speed until frothy. Slowly add granulated sugar, beating at medium-high speed until almost firm (but not stiff) peaks form. Fold one third of egg whites into chocolate mixture until blended. Gently fold in remaining egg whites just until blended. Spread batter in prepared pan; smooth top.

4 Pour water into Instant Pot; place rack in pot. Place pan on rack. Secure lid and move pressure release valve to Sealing position. Press Pressure Cook or Manual; cook at high pressure 15 minutes.

5 When cooking is complete, use natural release for 10 minutes, then release remaining pressure. Remove pan from pot. Cool in pan on wire rack 30 minutes; refrigerate at least 2 hours before serving. Remove side of pan; garnish with powdered sugar and raspberries.

Poached Autumn Fruit

Makes 4 to 6 servings

1	orange, peeled and halved
2½	to 3 cups water
½	cup dried cranberries
¼	cup sugar
2	tablespoons honey
1	teaspoon vanilla
1	whole cinnamon stick
2	Granny Smith apples, peeled and halved
2	Bartlett pears, peeled and quartered
	Vanilla ice cream (optional)

1 Squeeze juice from orange halves into Instant Pot; place orange halves in pot. Add 2½ cups water, cranberries, sugar, honey, vanilla and cinnamon stick; mix well. Add apples and pears; stir to coat. (Liquid should just cover fruit; if fruit is not covered, add additional water to cover.)

2 Secure lid and move pressure release valve to Sealing position. Press Pressure Cook or Manual; cook at high pressure 1 minute.

3 When cooking is complete, use quick release. Remove apples and pears to plate with slotted spoon; let stand until cool enough to handle.

4 Meanwhile, press Sauté; cook about 10 minutes or until liquid is reduced by one third and thickens slightly. Discard orange halves and cinnamon stick. Pour liquid through fine-mesh strainer into medium bowl; return to pot.

5 Cut apple and pears into 1-inch pieces. Return fruit to pot; stir gently to coat. Serve with ice cream, if desired.

Spiced Chocolate Bread Pudding

Makes 6 to 8 servings

1½ cups whipping cream

4 ounces unsweetened chocolate, coarsely chopped

2 eggs

½ cup sugar

1 teaspoon vanilla

¾ teaspoon ground cinnamon, plus additional for garnish

½ teaspoon ground allspice

⅛ teaspoon salt

3 cups cubed Hawaiian-style sweet bread, challah or brioche bread (½-inch cubes)

½ cup currants

1¼ cups water

Whipped cream (optional)

1 Spray 6- to 7-inch (1½-quart) soufflé dish or round baking dish with nonstick cooking spray. Heat cream to a simmer in medium saucepan over medium heat. Remove from heat. Add chocolate; stir until melted and smooth.

2 Beat eggs in large bowl. Add sugar, vanilla, ¾ teaspoon cinnamon, allspice and salt; mix well. Add chocolate mixture; stir until well blended. Add bread cubes and currants; stir gently to coat. Pour into prepared soufflé dish; cover with foil.

3 Pour water into Instant Pot; place rack in pot. Place soufflé dish on rack. Secure lid and move pressure release valve to Sealing position. Press Pressure Cook or Manual; cook at high pressure 35 minutes.

4 When cooking is complete, use natural release for 10 minutes, then release remaining pressure. Remove soufflé dish from pot. Uncover; serve warm or at room temperature. Top with whipped cream and additional cinnamon, if desired.

Sunshine Lemon Pie

Makes 8 servings

1 cup graham cracker crumbs

1 tablespoon sugar

2 tablespoons butter, melted

4 egg yolks

1 can (14 ounces) sweetened condensed milk

1/3 cup lemon juice

1/4 cup sour cream

1½ tablespoons grated lemon peel, plus additional for garnish

1 cup water

Fresh blueberries and/or whipped cream (optional)

1 Spray 7-inch springform pan with nonstick cooking spray. Combine graham cracker crumbs and sugar in small bowl; mix well. Stir in butter until well blended. Use bottom of glass or measuring cup to press mixture evenly into bottom of prepared pan. Place crust in freezer while preparing filling.

2 Beat egg yolks in large bowl until lightened in color. Slowly add sweetened condensed milk, beating until thickened. Add lemon juice, sour cream and 1½ tablespoons lemon peel; beat until well blended. Pour into crust. Cover pan with foil.

3 Pour water into Instant Pot; place rack in pot. Place pan on rack. Secure lid and move pressure release valve to Sealing position. Press Pressure Cook or Manual; cook at high pressure 20 minutes.

4 When cooking is complete, use natural release for 10 minutes, then release remaining pressure. Remove pan from pot. Uncover; blot any condensation on top of pie with paper towel, if necessary. Cool to room temperature. Cover and refrigerate at least 4 hours or overnight.

5 Remove side of pan. Garnish with additional lemon peel, blueberries and/or whipped cream.

Peanut Butter Pie
Makes 8 servings

- 10 chocolate crème-filled sandwich cookies, crushed into fine crumbs
- 1½ tablespoons butter, melted
- ⅔ cup creamy peanut butter
- ½ cup plus 2 tablespoons whipping cream, divided
- 2 eggs
- ⅓ cup whole milk
- ¼ cup packed brown sugar
- ½ teaspoon salt
- ½ teaspoon vanilla
- ⅓ cup plus ¼ cup semisweet chocolate chips, divided
- 1½ cups water
- 2 to 3 tablespoons chopped roasted salted peanuts

1 Spray 7-inch springform pan with nonstick cooking spray. Combine crushed cookies and butter in small bowl; mix well. Use bottom of glass or measuring cup to press mixture evenly into bottom of prepared pan. Place crust in freezer while preparing filling.

2 Whisk peanut butter, ½ cup cream, eggs, milk, brown sugar, salt and vanilla in medium bowl until well blended. Sprinkle ⅓ cup chocolate chips over bottom of crust. Pour peanut butter mixture over chocolate chips. Cover pan with foil.

3 Pour water into Instant Pot; place rack in pot. Place pan on rack. Secure lid and move pressure release valve to Sealing position. Press Pressure Cook or Manual; cook at high pressure 34 minutes.

4 When cooking is complete, use natural release for 10 minutes, then release remaining pressure. Remove pan from pot. Uncover; cool to room temperature. Cover and refrigerate at least 4 hours or overnight.

5 Heat remaining 2 tablespoons cream to a simmer in microwave or in small saucepan over low heat. Add remaining ¼ cup chocolate chips; stir until melted and smooth. Remove side of pan. Sprinkle peanuts over pie; drizzle with chocolate glaze.

Fudgy Double Chocolate Brownies

Makes 8 servings

½ cup (1 stick) butter

¾ cup unsweetened cocoa powder

1 cup sugar

2 eggs

⅔ cup all-purpose flour

½ teaspoon salt

½ cup semisweet chocolate chunks or chips

1½ cups water

Vanilla ice cream (optional)

1 Spray 7-inch metal cake pan with nonstick cooking spray. Line bottom of pan with parchment paper; spray with cooking spray. Place butter in medium microwavable bowl; microwave until melted. Stir in cocoa until well blended.

2 Beat sugar and eggs in large bowl until well blended. Add cocoa mixture; stir until smooth. Add flour and salt; stir until blended. Stir in chocolate chips. Spread batter in prepared pan; smooth top. Cover pan with paper towel (to absorb moisture), making sure paper towel does not touch batter. Cover pan with foil over paper towel.

3 Pour water into Instant Pot; place rack in pot. Place pan on rack. Secure lid and move pressure release valve to Sealing position. Press Pressure Cook or Manual; cook at high pressure 25 minutes.

4 When cooking is complete, use natural release for 10 minutes, then release remaining pressure. Remove pan from pot. Uncover; cool on wire rack at least 10 minutes before serving. Serve warm or at room temperature with ice cream, if desired.

Superfast Applesauce

Makes 4 cups

2 pounds (about 4 medium) sweet apples (such as Fuji, Gala or Honeycrisp), peeled and cut into 1-inch pieces

2 pounds (about 4 medium) Granny Smith apples, peeled and cut into 1-inch pieces

⅓ cup water

2 to 4 tablespoons packed brown sugar, divided

1 tablespoon lemon juice

1 teaspoon ground cinnamon

⅛ teaspoon salt

⅛ teaspoon ground nutmeg

⅛ teaspoon ground cloves

1 Combine apples, water, 2 tablespoons brown sugar, lemon juice, cinnamon, salt, nutmeg and cloves in Instant Pot; mix well.

2 Secure lid and move pressure release valve to Sealing position. Press Pressure Cook or Manual; cook at high pressure 4 minutes.

3 When cooking is complete, use quick release.

4 Stir applesauce; taste for seasoning and add remaining 2 tablespoons brown sugar, if desired. If there is excess liquid in pot, press Sauté and cook 2 to 3 minutes or until liquid evaporates. Cool completely before serving.

Chocolate Cheesecake

Makes 8 servings

22 chocolate crème-filled sandwich cookies

¼ cup (½ stick) butter, melted

¼ cup seedless raspberry jam

3 tablespoons whipping cream

1 teaspoon instant coffee granules or espresso powder (optional)

½ cup semisweet chocolate chips *or* 3 ounces chopped bittersweet chocolate

1½ packages (8 ounces each) cream cheese, softened

½ cup sugar

2 eggs

½ teaspoon vanilla

1¼ cups water

Whipped cream and fresh raspberries (optional)

1 Wrap outside of 7-inch springform pan with heavy-duty foil. Place cookies in food processor; process until finely ground. With motor running, drizzle in butter; process until well blended. Press mixture firmly into bottom of prepared pan. Spread jam over crust. Place crust in refrigerator while preparing filling.

2 Heat cream and coffee granules, if desired, in small saucepan until bubbles form around edge of pan. Remove from heat; add chocolate and let stand 2 minutes. Stir until well blended and smooth. Cool slightly.

3 Beat cream cheese in large bowl with electric mixer at medium-high speed until smooth. Add sugar; beat until light and fluffy. Add eggs, one at a time, beating well after each addition. Add vanilla and melted chocolate mixture; beat at low speed just until blended. Spread in prepared crust. (Pan should not be filled higher than ½ inch from top.) Cover pan tightly with foil.

4 Pour water into Instant Pot; place rack in pot. Place pan on rack. Secure lid and move pressure release valve to Sealing position. Press Pressure Cook or Manual; cook at high pressure 45 minutes.

5 When cooking is complete, use quick release. Remove pan from pot. Uncover; cool 1 hour. Run thin knife around edge of cheesecake to loosen (do not remove side of pan). Refrigerate 2 to 3 hours or overnight.

6 Remove side of pan. Garnish with whipped cream and raspberries.

Pumpkin Bread Pudding

Makes 4 servings

1 cup whole milk

2 eggs

½ cup canned pumpkin

⅓ cup packed brown sugar

1 tablespoon butter, melted

1½ teaspoons ground cinnamon

1 teaspoon vanilla

¼ teaspoon salt

¼ teaspoon ground nutmeg

8 slices cinnamon raisin bread, torn into small pieces (about 4 cups)

1¼ cups water

Bourbon Caramel Sauce (recipe follows, optional)

1 Spray 6- to 7-inch (1½-quart) soufflé dish or round baking dish with nonstick cooking spray. Whisk milk, eggs, pumpkin, brown sugar, butter, cinnamon, vanilla, salt and nutmeg in large bowl until well blended. Add bread cubes; stir gently to coat. Pour into prepared soufflé dish. Cover dish with foil.

2 Pour water into Instant Pot; place rack in pot. Place soufflé dish on rack. Secure lid and move pressure release valve to Sealing position. Press Pressure Cook or Manual; cook at high pressure 40 minutes.

3 When cooking is complete, use natural release for 10 minutes, then release remaining pressure.

4 Remove soufflé dish from pot. Uncover; cool 15 minutes. Meanwhile, prepare Bourbon Caramel Sauce, if desired. Serve bread pudding warm with sauce.

Bourbon Caramel Sauce

Combine ¼ cup (½ stick) butter, ¼ cup packed brown sugar and ¼ cup whipping cream in small saucepan; bring to a boil over high heat, stirring frequently. Remove from heat; stir in 1 tablespoon bourbon.

Chocolate Bundt Cake

Makes 8 servings

¾ cup boiling water

½ cup unsweetened cocoa powder

½ teaspoon espresso powder or instant coffee granules

1¼ cups all-purpose flour

1 teaspoon baking soda

½ teaspoon salt

¼ teaspoon baking powder

1¼ cups sugar

2 eggs

½ teaspoon vanilla

½ cup vegetable oil

⅓ cup sour cream

1½ cups water

¼ cup whipping cream

½ cup bittersweet or semisweet chocolate chips

1 Spray 6-cup bundt pan with nonstick cooking spray. Combine ¾ cup boiling water, cocoa and espresso powder in small bowl or measuring cup; whisk until smooth. Set aside to cool slightly.

2 Combine flour, baking soda, salt and baking powder in medium bowl; mix well. Whisk sugar, eggs and vanilla in large bowl until well blended. Stir in oil and sour cream; mix well. Add flour mixture; stir until blended. Add cocoa mixture; stir just until blended. Pour batter into prepared pan. Cover pan with foil.

3 Pour 1½ cups water into Instant Pot; place rack in pot. Place pan on rack. Secure lid and move pressure release valve to Sealing position. Press Pressure Cook or Manual; cook at high pressure 27 minutes.

4 When cooking is complete, use natural release for 10 minutes, then release remaining pressure. Remove pan from pot. Uncover; let stand 10 minutes. Invert cake onto serving plate; cool completely.

5 Heat cream to a simmer in microwave or in small saucepan over low heat. Add chocolate chips; stir until melted and smooth. Drizzle glaze over cake.

Carrot Cake
Makes 8 servings

1 cup all-purpose flour

1 teaspoon baking soda

1 teaspoon ground cinnamon

¼ teaspoon salt

⅔ cup granulated sugar

½ cup vegetable oil

2 eggs

1 teaspoon vanilla

1½ cups grated carrots (about 3 medium)

½ cup chopped walnuts or pecans

1½ cups water

2 ounces cream cheese, softened

¼ cup powdered sugar

2 to 3 tablespoons milk

1 Spray 6-cup bundt pan with nonstick cooking spray. Combine flour, baking soda, cinnamon and salt in small bowl; mix well.

2 Whisk granulated sugar, oil, eggs and vanilla in medium bowl until well blended. Add flour mixture; stir just until blended. Add carrots and walnuts; stir until blended. Pour batter into prepared pan. Cover pan with foil.

3 Pour water into Instant Pot; place rack in pot. Place pan on rack. Secure lid and move pressure release valve to Sealing position. Press Pressure Cook or Manual; cook at high pressure 37 minutes.

4 When cooking is complete, use natural release for 10 minutes, then release remaining pressure. Remove pan from pot. Uncover; let stand 10 minutes. Invert cake onto serving plate; cool completely.

5 Beat cream cheese in small bowl until smooth. (A hand mixer is best as quantities are too small for most stand mixers.) Add powdered sugar; beat until smooth. Beat in 2 tablespoons milk until blended. Add additional milk, 1 teaspoon at a time, if necessary to reach desired consistency. Drizzle glaze over cake. Let stand until set.

Southern Sweet Potato Custard

Makes 4 servings

1 can (16 ounces) cut sweet
   potatoes, drained
1 can (12 ounces) evaporated
   milk, divided
½ cup packed brown sugar
2 eggs
1 teaspoon ground cinnamon
½ teaspoon ground ginger
¼ teaspoon salt
1¼ cups water
   Whipped cream (optional)
   Ground nutmeg (optional)

1 Combine sweet potatoes and ¼ cup evaporated milk in food processor or blender; process until smooth. Add remaining milk, brown sugar, eggs, cinnamon, ginger and salt; process until well blended. Pour into 6- to 7-inch (1½-quart) soufflé dish. Cover dish with foil.

2 Pour water into Instant Pot; place rack in pot. Place soufflé dish on rack. Secure lid and move pressure release valve to Sealing position. Press Pressure Cook or Manual; cook at high pressure 40 minutes.

3 When cooking is complete, use natural release for 10 minutes, then release remaining pressure.

4 Remove soufflé dish from pot. Uncover; let stand 30 minutes. Garnish with whipped cream and nutmeg.

Fudgy Chocolate Pudding Cake

Makes 6 servings

¾ cup plus ⅓ cup granulated sugar, divided

1 cup all-purpose flour

¼ cup plus 3 tablespoons unsweetened cocoa powder, divided

2 teaspoons baking powder

¼ teaspoon salt

½ cup milk

⅓ cup butter, melted

1 teaspoon vanilla

½ cup packed brown sugar

1 cup hot water

1¼ cups water

Vanilla ice cream (optional)

1 Spray 6- to 7-inch (1½-quart) soufflé dish or round baking dish with nonstick cooking spray.

2 Combine ¾ cup granulated sugar, flour, ¼ cup cocoa, baking powder and salt in medium bowl; mix well. Add milk, butter and vanilla; whisk until well blended. Spread batter in prepared soufflé dish; smooth top. Combine brown sugar, remaining ⅓ cup granulated sugar and 3 tablespoons cocoa in small bowl; mix well. Sprinkle evenly over batter. Pour 1 cup hot water over top. *Do not stir.*

3 Pour 1¼ cups water into Instant Pot; place rack in pot. Place soufflé dish on rack. Secure lid and move pressure release valve to Sealing position. Press Pressure Cook or Manual; cook at high pressure 40 minutes.

4 When cooking is complete, use natural release for 10 minutes, then release remaining pressure. Remove soufflé dish from pot; let stand 5 minutes. Serve warm with ice cream, if desired.

Quick and Easy Kheer (Indian Rice Pudding)

Makes 6 to 8 servings

3 cups whole milk

⅔ cup sugar

1 cup uncooked basmati rice, rinsed and drained

½ cup golden raisins

3 whole green cardamom pods *or* ¼ teaspoon ground cardamon

¼ teaspoon salt

Grated orange peel (optional)

Pistachio nuts (optional)

1 Combine milk and sugar in Instant Pot; stir until sugar is dissolved. Add rice, raisins, cardamom and salt; mix well.

2 Secure lid and move pressure release valve to Sealing position. Press Pressure Cook or Manual; cook at high pressure 5 minutes.

3 When cooking is complete, use natural release for 10 minutes, then release remaining pressure.

4 Stir rice pudding well before serving. (Pudding will thicken upon standing.) Garnish with orange peel and pistachios.

Magic Chocoflan

Makes about 10 servings

⅓ cup caramel ice cream topping or caramel sauce

Cake

¾ cup all-purpose flour

¼ cup unsweetened cocoa powder

½ teaspoon baking soda

½ teaspoon baking powder

½ teaspoon espresso powder

¼ teaspoon salt

⅓ cup butter, softened

½ cup sugar

1 egg

½ cup buttermilk

Flan

½ (14-ounce) can sweetened condensed milk

½ (12-ounce) can evaporated milk

2 eggs

½ teaspoon vanilla

1½ cups water

1 Spray 6-cup bundt pan with nonstick cooking spray. Spread caramel topping in even layer in bottom of pan.

2 For cake, combine flour, cocoa, baking soda, baking powder, espresso powder and salt in small bowl. Beat butter and sugar in medium bowl with electric mixer at medium speed about 3 minutes or until light and fluffy, scraping down side of bowl several times. Add 1 egg; beat until well blended. Alternately add flour mixture and buttermilk in two additions, beating just until blended. *Do not overbeat.*

3 For flan, combine evaporated milk, sweetened condensed milk, 2 eggs and vanilla in blender; blend about 1 minute or until smooth. Spoon cake batter into prepared pan over caramel layer; spread evenly and smooth top. Slowly pour flan mixture over cake batter.

4 Pour water into Instant Pot; place rack in pot. Place pan on rack. Secure lid and move pressure release valve to Sealing position. Cook at high pressure 17 minutes.

5 When cooking is complete, use natural release for 15 minutes, then release remaining pressure. Remove pan from pot. Cool to room temperature on wire rack.

6 Place serving plate over pan; invert chocoflan onto plate. Scrape any caramel left in pan onto top of chocoflan.

Irish Soda Bread Pudding

Makes 8 servings

1 loaf (about 12 ounces)
   Irish soda bread,
   cut into 1-inch cubes
   (about 5 cups)

1 cup whole milk

3 eggs

½ cup whipping cream

¼ cup sugar

⅛ teaspoon salt

1 medium Jonagold,
   Braeburn or Fuji apple,
   peeled and cut into
   ¾-inch cubes
   (about 1 cup)

1 package (6 ounces)
   fresh blackberries

1½ cups water

1 Preheat oven to 375°F.* Spray 6- to 7-inch (1½-quart) soufflé dish or round baking dish that fits inside Instant Pot with nonstick cooking spray. Spread bread cubes on baking sheet; bake 8 to 10 minutes or until lightly toasted, stirring halfway through baking time.

2 Whisk milk, eggs, cream, sugar and salt in medium bowl until well blended. Transfer half of bread cubes to prepared soufflé dish; sprinkle with half of apple and half of blackberries. Top with remaining bread cubes, then remaining fruit. Pour milk mixture over fruit and bread; press down gently to submerge in liquid. Let stand 10 minutes. Cover dish with foil.

3 Pour water into pot; place rack in pot. Place baking dish on rack. Secure lid and move pressure release valve to Sealing position. Press Pressure Cook or Manual; cook at high pressure 40 minutes.

4 When cooking is complete, use natural release for 5 minutes, then release remaining pressure. Remove soufflé dish from pot. Uncover; cool to room temperature. Cut into wedges.

If using bread that is dry or stale, you can skip the toasting step. Fresh bread should be toasted before using in the recipe.

Chocolate Surprise Crème Brûlée

Makes 5 servings

3 ounces bittersweet chocolate, finely chopped

5 egg yolks

1¾ cups whipping cream

½ cup granulated sugar

¼ teaspoon salt

1 teaspoon vanilla

1 cup water

¼ cup demerara or raw sugar

1 Spray bottoms of five 6-ounce ramekins or custard cups with nonstick cooking spray. Divide chocolate evenly among ramekins.

2 Whisk egg yolks in medium bowl. Combine cream, granulated sugar and salt in medium saucepan; bring to a simmer over medium heat. Slowly pour ¼ cup hot cream mixture into egg yolks, whisking until blended. Add remaining cream mixture in thin, steady stream, whisking constantly. Pour through fine-mesh strainer into clean bowl. Stir in vanilla. Ladle custard mixture into prepared ramekins over chocolate. Cover each ramekin with foil.

3 Pour water into Instant Pot; place rack in pot. Arrange ramekins on rack, stacking as necessary.

4 Secure lid and move pressure release valve to Sealing position. Press Pressure Cook or Manual; cook at high pressure 6 minutes. When cooking is complete, use natural release for 10 minutes, then release remaining pressure. Remove ramekins from pot. Uncover; cool to room temperature. Refrigerate until ready to serve.

5 Just before serving, preheat broiler. Place ramekins on baking sheet; sprinkle tops of custards with demerara sugar. Broil 4 inches from heat 1 to 2 minutes or until sugar bubbles and browns.

Espresso Crème Brûlée

Reduce cream to 1½ cups and add ¼ cup espresso. Heat mixture in saucepan with granulated sugar and salt as directed in step 2.

PRESSURE COOKING TIMES

MEAT

MEAT	MINUTES UNDER PRESSURE	PRESSURE	RELEASE
Beef, Bone-in Short Ribs	35 to 45	High	Natural
Beef, Brisket	60 to 75	High	Natural
Beef, Ground	8	High	Natural
Beef, Roast (round, rump or shoulder)	60 to 70	High	Natural
Beef, Stew Meat	20 to 25	High	Natural or Quick
Lamb, Chops	5 to 10	High	Quick
Lamb, Leg or Shanks	35 to 40	High	Natural
Lamb, Stew Meat	12 to 15	High	Quick
Pork, Baby Back Ribs	25 to 30	High	Natural
Pork, Chops	7 to 10	High	Quick
Pork, Ground	5	High	Quick
Pork, Loin	15 to 25	High	Natural
Pork, Shoulder or Butt	45 to 60	High	Natural
Pork, Stew Meat	15 to 20	High	Quick

POULTRY

POULTRY	MINUTES UNDER PRESSURE	PRESSURE	RELEASE
Chicken Breasts, Bone-in	7 to 10	High	Quick
Chicken Breasts, Boneless	5 to 8	High	Quick
Chicken Thigh, Bone-in	10 to 14	High	Natural
Chicken Thigh, Boneless	8 to 10	High	Natural
Chicken Wings	10 to 12	High	Quick

Chicken, Whole	22 to 26	High	Natural
Eggs, Hard-Cooked (3 to 12)	9	Low	Quick
Turkey Breast, Bone-in	25 to 30	High	Natural
Turkey Breast, Boneless	15 to 20	High	Natural
Turkey Legs	35 to 40	High	Natural
Turkey, Ground	8 to 10	High	Quick

SEAFOOD

SEAFOOD	MINUTES UNDER PRESSURE	PRESSURE	RELEASE
Cod	2 to 3	Low	Quick
Crab	2 to 3	Low	Quick
Halibut	6	Low	Quick
Mussels	1 to 2	Low	Quick
Salmon	4 to 5	Low	Quick
Scallops	1	Low	Quick
Shrimp	2 to 3	Low	Quick
Swordfish	4 to 5	Low	Quick
Tilapia	3	Low	Quick

DRIED BEANS AND LEGUMES

DRIED BEANS AND LEGUMES	UNSOAKED	SOAKED	PRESSURE	RELEASE
Black Beans	22 to 25	8 to 10	High	Natural
Black-Eyed Peas	9 to 11	3 to 5	High	Natural
Cannellini Beans	30 to 35	8 to 10	High	Natural
Chickpeas	35 to 40	18 to 22	High	Natural
Great Northern Beans	25 to 30	7 to 10	High	Natural

Instant Pot

Kidney Beans	20 to 25	8 to 12	High	Natural
Lentils, Brown or Green	10 to 12	n/a	High	Natural
Lentils, Red or Yellow Split	1	n/a	High	Natural
Navy Beans	20 to 25	7 to 8	High	Natural
Pinto Beans	22 to 25	8 to 10	High	Natural
Split Peas	8 to 10	n/a	High	Natural

GRAINS	LIQUID PER CUP	MINUTES UNDER PRESSURE	PRESSURE	RELEASE
Barley, Pearl	2	18 to 22	High	Natural
Barley, Whole	2½	30 to 35	High	Natural
Bulgur	3	8	High	Natural
Farro	2	10 to 12	High	Natural
Grits, Medium	4	12 to 15	High	10 minute natural
Millet	1½	1	High	Natural
Oats, Rolled	2	4 to 5	High	10 minute natural
Oats, Steel-Cut	3	10 to 13	High	10 minute natural
Quinoa	1½	1	High	10 minute natural
Polenta, Instant	3	5	High	5 minute natural
Rice, Arborio	2	6 to 7	High	Quick
Rice, Brown	1	22	High	10 minute natural
Rice, White Long Grain	1	4	High	10 minute natural

VEGETABLES	MINUTES UNDER PRESSURE	PRESSURE	RELEASE
Artichokes, Whole	9 to 12	High	Natural
Beets, Medium Whole	18 to 24	High	Quick
Brussels Sprouts, Whole	2 to 3	High	Quick

Cabbage, Sliced	3 to 5	High	Quick
Carrots, Sliced	2 to 4	High	Quick
Cauliflower, Florets	2 to 3	High	Quick
Cauliflower, Whole	3 to 5	High	Quick
Corn on the Cob	2 to 4	High	Quick
Eggplant	3 to 4	High	Quick
Fennel, Sliced	3 to 4	High	Quick
Green Beans	2 to 4	High	Quick
Kale	3	High	Quick
Leeks	3	High	Quick
Okra	3	High	Quick
Potatoes, Baby or Fingerling	6 to 10	High	Natural
Potatoes, New	7 to 9	High	Natural
Potatoes, 1-inch pieces	4 to 6	High	Quick
Potatoes, Sweet, 1-inch pieces	3	High	Quick
Potatoes, Sweet, Whole	8 to 12	High	Natural
Spinach	1	High	Quick
Squash, Acorn, Halved	7	High	Natural
Squash, Butternut, 1-inch pieces	4 to 6	High	Quick
Squash, Spaghetti, Halved	6 to 10	High	Natural
Tomatoes, cut into pieces for sauce	5	High	Natural

Instant Pot

METRIC CONVERSION CHART

VOLUME MEASUREMENTS (dry)

1/8 teaspoon = 0.5 mL
1/4 teaspoon = 1 mL
1/2 teaspoon = 2 mL
3/4 teaspoon = 4 mL
1 teaspoon = 5 mL
1 tablespoon = 15 mL
2 tablespoons = 30 mL
1/4 cup = 60 mL
1/3 cup = 75 mL
1/2 cup = 125 mL
2/3 cup = 150 mL
3/4 cup = 175 mL
1 cup = 250 mL
2 cups = 1 pint = 500 mL
3 cups = 750 mL
4 cups = 1 quart = 1 L

VOLUME MEASUREMENTS (fluid)

1 fluid ounce (2 tablespoons) = 30 mL
4 fluid ounces (1/2 cup) = 125 mL
8 fluid ounces (1 cup) = 250 mL
12 fluid ounces (1 1/2 cups) = 375 mL
16 fluid ounces (2 cups) = 500 mL

WEIGHTS (mass)

1/2 ounce = 15 g
1 ounce = 30 g
3 ounces = 90 g
4 ounces = 120 g
8 ounces = 225 g
10 ounces = 285 g
12 ounces = 360 g
16 ounces = 1 pound = 450 g

DIMENSIONS

1/16 inch = 2 mm
1/8 inch = 3 mm
1/4 inch = 6 mm
1/2 inch = 1.5 cm
3/4 inch = 2 cm
1 inch = 2.5 cm

OVEN TEMPERATURES

250°F = 120°C
275°F = 140°C
300°F = 150°C
325°F = 160°C
350°F = 180°C
375°F = 190°C
400°F = 200°C
425°F = 220°C
450°F = 230°C

BAKING PAN SIZES

Utensil	Size in Inches/Quarts	Metric Volume	Size in Centimeters
Baking or Cake Pan (square or rectangular)	8×8×2	2 L	20×20×5
	9×9×2	2.5 L	23×23×5
	12×8×2	3 L	30×20×5
	13×9×2	3.5 L	33×23×5
Loaf Pan	8×4×3	1.5 L	20×10×7
	9×5×3	2 L	23×13×7
Round Layer Cake Pan	8×1½	1.2 L	20×4
	9×1½	1.5 L	23×4
Pie Plate	8×1¼	750 mL	20×3
	9×1¼	1 L	23×3
Baking Dish or Casserole	1 quart	1 L	—
	1½ quart	1.5 L	—
	2 quart	2 L	—